praise for *the*

D0456724

"Janet Conner has emerged as a vibrant and innovative spiritual teacher. In her new book, *The Lotus and the Lily,* Janet unlocks vital secrets to manifestation. She has created a process that helps people create their relationship to the divine and set the stage to receive what we desire in alignment with our highest good. She teaches a myriad of techniques, including an unusual way to use the mandala. My mandala reminds me daily of staying connected to my trusted source and keeps me centered on the importance of creating a receptive context. Janet has a key piece of the spiritual puzzle—this book will move you way ahead on your spiritual journey."

—Gail McMeekin, author of *The 12 Secrets of Highly Successful Women* and *The 12 Secrets of Highly Creative Women*

"*The Lotus and the Lily* is a healthy corrective for the ego-driven, materialistic interpretation of spirituality that is epidemic in our culture. Spirituality is not about getting your stuff. It is about developing a closer relationship with the Transcendent, however named, as Janet Conner makes clear."

—Larry Dossey, MD, author of *Healing Words* and *The Power of Premonitions*

"The principles that Janet Conner guides the reader to discover become the essential elements of a dynamic spiritual practice. These principles transcend denomination and dogma. They are practical, universal, and impacting."

—Mary Anne Radmacher, artist and author of *Live with Intention* and *Lean Forward into Your Life*

"Jesus said we could create heaven on earth. The Buddha said we could create the conditions for manifestation. Janet Conner tells us *how*. Her 30-day program is spiritual yet eminently practical, deeply serious yet lots of fun. This is a step-by-step guide to expressing our own divinity."

—Ellen Debenport, author of *The Five Principles*

"Janet Conner has her priorities straight. And because she does, she's written a poetically precise guide to how we can all grow beyond 'What's in it for me?' to 'Just how do I seek first the kingdom?' Do what she says and you'll know what it means to have 'all these things' added to your very blessed life."

—Victoria Moran, HHC, AADA, author of
Creating a Charmed Life and *Main Street Vegan*

"Janet Connor has taken her readers from *Writing Down Your Soul* to fully aligning with the pure intentions of our purpose on earth. Janet's book, *The Lotus and the Lily*, lifts, lightens, and leads the dedicated truth student to understanding true prosperity. Lasting prosperity is when the lower earth chakras are balanced and the heart chakra is open to allow the upper chakras of heaven to be revealed. The 'I AM' expression along with the gift of inner seeing lead the readers to a new way of existence—a life free of wanting and a joyful life of always having."

—Rev. Temple Hayes, senior minister of Unity Campus,
St. Petersburg, FL, and author of
How to Speak Unity and *The Right to Be You*

"I believe there is no more important work we do than culturing our inner knowing. As a lifetime journal keeper, I have chosen Janet Conner to be my most trusted guide on my interior journey. Revealing secret paths and signposts, she illuminates our deepest and most fulfilling ways of being and becoming. Through *The Lotus and The Lily* I learned to plant the seeds of my intention for a beautiful life in the fields of my Soul. A bountiful harvest awaits all who journey within."

—Diana von Welanetz Wentworth, founder of the Inside Edge motivational breakfast forum (www.InsideEdge.org), and author of nine bestselling and award-winning books including two titles in the bestselling Chicken Soup for the Soul series

"In this deeply nourishing 30-day program, Janet Conner weaves a magic carpet of the combined paradoxical wisdom of Buddha and Jesus and carries us into transcendent creativity. *The Lotus and The Lily* is a joy ride!"

—Ted Wentworth, author of *The Enlightenment Code* and editor-in-chief of *Enlightenment Lifestyle Magazine*

"*The Lotus and The Lily* is simply divine. In it, Janet Conner takes us far beyond the Law of Attraction. Through her deeply transformative process, we learn to prepare ourselves for the life of our dreams. After participating in Janet's program, I experienced a shift in focus—from wants and worries to creating the conditions for my life to flourish. This shift made all the difference."

—Laura Harvey, editor of *Daily Word*

"*The Lotus and the Lily* is an invitation to experience more of everything that life has to offer. Wise, warm, and friendly, this is an essential guide to living the adventure of your soul."

—Joel Fotinos, author of *Think and Grow Rich Every Day*

the lotus
and the lily

*Access the Wisdom of Buddha and Jesus
to Nourish Your Beautiful, Abundant Life*

JANET CONNER

Conari Press

First published in 2012 by Conari Press
Red Wheel/Weiser, LLC
with offices at:
665 Third Street, Suite 400
San Francisco, CA 94107
www.redwheelweiser.com

ISBN: 978-1-57324-586-9

Library of Congress Cataloging-in-Publication Data available upon
   request

Cover design by Jim Warner
Cover photograph © VonHenry Media, Inc.
Graphics by Sandy Cromp, Sunshine Design Studio
Text design by Jane Hagaman
Typeset in Mrs Eaves and Gill Sans Std

Printed in the United States of America
VG

10 9 8 7 6 5 4 3 2 1

The paper used in this publication meets the minimum requirements of
the American National Standard for Information Sciences—Permanence
of Paper for Printed Library Materials Z39.48-1992 (R1997).

For you,

because your soul wants five things

and one of them is to

create life

Ever since Happiness heard your name,
It has been running through the streets
Trying to find you.
And several times in the last week,
God Himself has come to my door—
So sweetly asking for your address,
Wanting the beautiful warmth of your heart's fire.

—Hafiz, from "Several Times in the Last Week,"
I Heard God Laughing, translation by Daniel Ladinsky

They are like shy, young school kids—time and space,
before the woman and the man who are
intimate with God.

The realized soul can play with this universe
the way a child can a ball.

—St. Teresa of Avila, from "The Grail,"
Love Poems from God, translation by Daniel Ladinsky

contents

our master teachers

The Lotus

This is because that is.

—The Buddha

When conditions are sufficient there is a manifestation.

—Thich Nhat Hanh, *You Are Here*

The Lily

But seek ye first the kingdom of God, and his righteousness; and all these things shall be added unto you.

—Jesus, Matthew 6:33 (King James Version)

Here Jesus says that when we pursue a right relationship with the Universal One and allow this relationship to realign our lives, we produce a condition of receptivity in which anything we need to help us complete our purpose in life will be supplied by the universe.

—Neil Douglas-Klotz, *Blessings of the Cosmos*

Note to Readers

This book is intended to be an informational guide and is not meant to treat, diagnose, or prescribe. Always consult with a qualified health care professional regarding any medical condition or symptoms. Neither the author nor the publisher accepts any responsibility for your health or how you choose to use the information contained in this book.

welcome

Welcome to the divine playground of your soul. Here, Julian of Norwich's sweet blessing "All shall be well, and all shall be well, and all manner of thing shall be well" actually comes to pass. And none too soon. For many of us things haven't been going so well. We look around and wonder, "What happened? How did I get here?"

It isn't that we haven't been told what to do. We have. In many ways and by many teachers, we've been told to ask and receive. Asking sounds so easy and so fun. And sometimes, it works! But sometimes, nothing happens. Or the wrong thing happens. So we ask again. And again. And again. It seems no matter how much activity there is at the asking end, there's never quite enough on the receiving end.

Something is wrong, and we assume it must be with us. Maybe we're not asking correctly, or we're not clear enough about what we want, or our thoughts aren't in the right alignment, or perhaps our vibration is off, or we don't trust enough, or we're not saying the right affirmations, or—here's a scary thought—maybe we don't deserve to get what we want. Or, yikes, what if the universe doesn't actually work this way.

It's frustrating to keep knocking at a door that doesn't seem to want to open. Many of us are ready to give up.

Please don't give up. There's nothing wrong with you, and there's nothing wrong with the way the universe works. Furthermore, you are utterly and completely worthy of experiencing a life of abundance and joy. And—here's an important piece of good news—you already possess everything you need to create that life. Because you are a soul. That means you were born with innate spiritual intelligence. That means direct and immediate access to the Divine was built into you at the factory. That means the creative powers of desire, imagination, will, and intention are all at your fingertips. Hafiz, the peerless Sufi mystic, knows this little secret about you:

> All the talents of God are within you.
> How could this be otherwise
> When your soul
> Derived from His
> Genes!

> —Hafiz, from "All the Talents of God," *The Gift,*
> translation by Daniel Ladinsky

Here's another little secret: You chose this human experience, and you came to live in beauty, not in pain—to consume life, not to be consumed by it. You came to create life, and at the soul level, you know how to do that. You've just humanly forgotten, as we all have. But the truth is still alive and waiting. The great masters, the Buddha and Jesus, told us ages ago how to create an abundant life and—guess what?—they did *not* say get clear about what you want and ask for it. The Buddha said, "When conditions are sufficient there is a manifestation." Jesus said, "[W]hen we pursue a right relationship with the Universal One and allow this relationship to realign our lives, we produce a condition of receptivity in which anything we need to help us complete our purpose in life will be supplied by the universe."

Although they lived six hundred years and thousands of miles apart, and gave birth to two very different spiritual traditions, the Buddha and Jesus taught exactly the same thing: you create a beautiful life by creating fertile conditions, not by asking for anything. In my own words, what I hear them saying is this: You can have anything you want—why, you can have things you don't even know you want—but not by focusing on them. Instead, put your undivided attention on your connection with the vibrant presence of the Divine within, and your life will change. It has to. It is the natural order.

Sound like a paradox? It is. It's the Great Paradox of Prosperity. Get used to paradox. It's one of the Divine's favorite games. So is creation. In *The Lotus and the Lily*, you will play with many creation toys. You will learn the cosmic power of the mandala. You will play with Soul Slinky waves of intention and gratitude. You will awaken your inner shaman and be amazed at what you can do. You will discover the power of naming your past and your future. And you will experience the generative power of your own voice.

It all sounds rather magical, but it isn't. It's natural order—the same natural order that produces an abundant harvest on a physical farm. A wise farmer will tell you that planting a seed takes a few seconds. The real value is in the preparation of the soil. Fertile fields produce lush crops. That abundant beautiful life you want? That's one very lush crop. So for the next twenty-eight days, you will walk your spiritual fields, plucking weeds, removing rocks, and nourishing your soil with twenty-eight essential spiritual truths. When the fields are ready, you will give yourself a special Soul Day. On that day, you will clarify your conditions and plant the seeds of your beautiful life in a highly charged and deeply personal Intention Mandala. Then you only have to watch what happens. Because when conditions are sufficient, there *will* be a manifestation.

These fields of the soul lie beyond our popular understanding of the law of attraction. This doesn't mean the law of attraction is wrong; it means that we've been limiting ourselves to one small corner of our creative capability. Why ask for one thing or another when you can create fertile conditions in which everything you need is supplied? Here's a comparison of the principles of Law of Attraction and those we'll be using:

Law of Attraction	The Lotus and the Lily
human at the center	divine at the center
how to ask	how to live
ask for things	create conditions
ego	soul
external	internal
desires	purpose
effort	effortless
control	allow
material goods	heaven on earth

Does heaven on earth sound implausible? It's not. The Buddha and Jesus pointed the way. All we have to do is follow.

Come. Out here, the pastures are beautiful and the harvest is rich. Out here, anything is possible. Out here, all the talents of your soul come out to play. Out here, all is well. More than well, all is divine. Everything is unfolding according to divine will. Welcome, you are on your way!

The Story Behind the Lotus and the Lily

I discovered the process described in this book the same way I discovered deep soul writing, which I introduced to readers in *Writing Down Your Soul*—on my knees. I stumbled onto deep soul writing trying to navigate a terrifying divorce. Out of sheer desperation, I picked up a pen and poured my woes onto the page. There, I made a startling discovery: the connection to Source is in your hands. You ask for guidance, and you receive it. It's that simple. Thousands of people have been making the connection ever since.

Thanks to *Writing Down Your Soul*, my career leapt from human-resources consultant to spiritual writer. This, I thought, was a very good thing. When my book came out in early 2009, I happily traipsed around the country teaching deep soul writing. Every day brought new stories of lives changed by the guidance and comfort received on the page. But those trips were financed on my already-burdened credit cards. By November, I had to face the reality that I was bankrupt. I sat down with my son and told him how ashamed I was to be in such a pickle. I couldn't even say the word *bankrupt;* it came out as a little sob. My son, Jerry, wise before his years, said, "Mom, there's nothing to be ashamed of. I'm proud of you. You're doing the work you want to do. If bankruptcy is the next step, take it." With his words the shame dissolved, and I called a bankruptcy attorney. But his first available appointment wasn't until the following February. What was I supposed to do till then?

The next morning, I said my prayers and got in my sacred writing chair. I told Spirit all about my financial woes and my loving son and the appointment with the attorney. I asked a lot of hard questions: Why, if I'm doing the work I'm here to do, am I broke? How did I get here? What am I supposed to be learning? Where's the blessing in bankruptcy? I want a beautiful life! I want real prosperity. How do I create that? Tell me how to create a beautiful life, and I will do it.

Well, I received answers. I was told to write at the very deepest soul level every day of December. And I was told exactly what to write about and in what order.

Week 1: Spend a week in preparation. Learning how to create life is deep; you need to prepare yourself.

Week 2: Look back at your life. There are gifts buried in there that you haven't explored and don't understand.

Week 3: Release and forgive. You are full of old wounds that haven't been released, and until you release them, there is no room for the new to grow.

Week 4: Before you ask for anything, get clear about what you want and why you want it, so you are sure to create a life of purpose and joy.

This outline made sense to me. In fact, it sounded similar to what I'd been doing on my annual Soul Day. Every New Year's Day, I'd spend time in prayerful preparation, then I'd write about the year just completed and all the gifts and learnings I received, and finally, I'd talk over what I want for the new year.

This process had always worked, but it had been wildly effective on January 1, 2006. That year, no matter what I asked for, I received it. I said I was ready for my marketing partner, and five days later, the news and information outlet United Press International (UPI) invited me to write a weekly column. I said I was ready for my publishing partner, and book publisher Conari Press contacted me in June. I asked for a relationship, and met a man thirteen days later in my favorite restaurant. That year, 2006, was far and away my most magical year to date. I wanted another year like *that*.

On January 1, 2010, after four weeks of intense spiritual exploration, I felt ready to call in a magical new year. That morning, I woke early, made a pot of coffee, and headed to my writing room. I said my prayers and settled in for a day of divine dialogue. But when I reached for my journal, I noticed a bright yellow book, *You Are Here,* by Thich Nhat Hanh, at my feet. I began to read and couldn't stop. Thich Nhat Hanh kept drawing me deeper and deeper into his book with his gentle, loving explanation of the Buddha's great teachings. In a chapter on how everything is connected, I turned the page and stumbled upon a sentence: "When conditions are sufficient there is a manifestation."

I stopped and read it again. Then I read it out loud. Then I leapt out of my chair. My hands shot to my forehead. I raced in circles around my room gushing, "Oh my God! Oh my

God! Everything we think we know about manifestation is 180 degrees *off!*" I ran to my white board and scribbled "When conditions are sufficient there is a manifestation" in green marker. I stared at the sentence, letting this deeper understanding of manifestation settle into my bones. Here I was, wanting to manifest a beautiful life, but I had my eyes on the wrong half of the equation. I was focused on what I wanted, but it's not about wanting. It's about creating the conditions that organically produce what I want. Conditions first; manifestation second. From the moment I read that sentence, my Soul Day changed forever. Heck, my whole life changed forever.

I spent the rest of the day alternating between reading *You Are Here* and talking over what I was learning with the Voice—what I call the speaker of the divine guidance that appears on the page when I'm soul writing. The Voice and I had rich conversations about the full implications of "when conditions are sufficient."

Suddenly, I wondered if this is what Jesus meant when he said, "Seek first the kingdom and God's righteousness and all else shall be provided" (Matthew 6:33). Surely the two great masters, the Buddha and Jesus, would have to have taught the same thing.

I jumped out of my chair and searched my bookshelves for *Blessings of the Cosmos* by Neil Douglas-Klotz. I knew from spending time with his earlier book, *Prayers of the Cosmos,* that Jesus spoke Aramaic, a rich Middle Eastern language that carries literal, metaphorical, and mystical meanings simultaneously. When the gospels were written in Greek and then translated into Latin and finally English, much of the majesty and impact of Jesus's words were washed out along the way. In *Blessings,* Douglas-Klotz says that in English we read, "Seek first the kingdom," but in Aramaic, Jesus's words are much more thrilling and clear. To give us a sense for what first-century Aramaic listeners heard, he translates "Seek first the kingdom" into a whole page of poetry. In the end, he captures Jesus's intent with this summary: "Here Jesus says that when we pursue a right relationship with the Universal One and allow this relationship to realign our lives, we produce a condition of receptivity in which anything we need to help us complete our purpose in life will be supplied by the universe."

With the wisdom of the two great masters stirring in my heart, I made an Intention Mandala for 2010. (Later in the book, I'll explain exactly what a mandala is, why it's important, and how an Intention Mandala fits into the Lotus and the Lily process.) It had pictures of what I wanted, but those images were on the periphery of the circular mandala, not the center. At the heart of my mandala, I drew a lily and on each petal wrote one of my conditions—the six actions I take every day to live a life aligned with Spirit and become the fertile soil in which my beautiful life can grow. Then I gave my mandala a name: "My Breakthrough Year."

I posted "My Breakthrough Year" on the wall and began a daily mandala prayer practice. Every morning, I stood in front of my mandala, handed my desires over to Spirit, and announced aloud that I would spend the day focusing on my part of the equation—living my conditions. I talked to my mandala every morning, and from its position overlooking my computer, it spoke to me all day.

Forty days later, I had my appointment with the bankruptcy attorney. He explained the process and asked if I had any questions. "One," I said, "I made $12,000 in January. Is that a problem?"

"Well, yeah, it's a problem," he said. "You're not bankrupt."

After the appointment, I drove to my favorite holy place, St. Michael's Shrine in Tarpon Springs, Florida. There, I poured tears of gratitude onto my soul-journal page, thanking the angels and Spirit for leading me to the teachings of the Buddha and Jesus. "How can I thank you?" I wrote. The answer was simple and clear: teach it. I've taught the process I discovered, which I call "the Lotus and the Lily," ever since.

And now, here you are.

How to Use This Book

This book, *The Lotus and the Lily*, will lead you on a dance with t
wisdom of your wild soul—the part of you that is authentic,
alive, and hungry for the full adventure of life. Your soul has
never been wounded and never can be. It emerged from divine
ground, and it will return to divine ground. In between, it is
here to play in the fields of life.

Most of us have only a cursory relationship with our brilliant soul. We hear occasional tapping on the window—perhaps
a nudge to explore an idea or ask a bigger question or consider
a new possibility. But we rarely sit down and say, "I'm here.
I'm listening. What do you want?" In *Writing Down Your Soul*, I
share what can happen when you step out of conscious mind
for a few moments and give the extraordinary Voice room to
speak. Now, here in *The Lotus and the Lily*, you will use deep soul
writing and many other delightful spiritual practices to give
your wild soul all the room it needs to create a truly beautiful
and abundant life.

There are thirty experiences, one each day. The first twenty-
eight are divided into four week-long explorations:

Week 1: Prepare—step into your natural spiritual power,
set your intention, and create your own ritual and prayer

Week 2: Look Back—uncover all the gifts in the life you've
created to date

Week 3: Create Space—make room for the new by releasing and forgiving the old

Week 4: Look Forward—identify what you want in alignment with your soul's desires

After twenty-eight days of rich exploration, you will spend
Day 29 setting up your Soul Day. And then, on Day 30, you will
give yourself something precious—a day alone with your soul. On
this day, you will clarify your all-important conditions. Then,

ns in hand, you will make a highly charged
al Intention Mandala. The mandala, as you
, not only holds everything you want, but it
to the universe to draw it all to you.

a sounds exciting, and it is, but don't jump
an͟ is a reason the days progress the way they do.
They build gently one upon the other until you know you are
ready for your Soul Day. Without the twenty-eight days of
preparation, you could create a life, but it might not be the
life you really want.

The Structure of Each Day

The Lotus and the Lily process is deep, but it is not work.
The soul does not work. At the soul level, life is divine play.
Approach the content of the day from the vantage point of
soul play, and you'll discover that even the deepest exploration can be a source of delight. Each day begins with a page
or two about the day's subject, then invites you to play in the
following ways:

Reflect. Big questions crack you open and allow big information to flow in. Ponder these questions before you dive
into your deep soul writing.

 Write. Each day has a sample deep-soul-writing prompt
to stimulate your imagination. Take any parts that speak
to you, but allow your own conversation to come through
your hands, onto the page.

Explore. Pick and choose any activities that call to you, or
create your own.

Nourish. This short, powerful, soul-nourishing statement holds the essence of the day. Savor it aloud. Feel
its wisdom enter your being. Write each statement on a
card or in your journal, and watch what happens as these
jewels accumulate.

Want More? If you want more, dive into any of the books and resources listed for additional information.

Paradox Alerts

As you walk through the Lotus and the Lily, you'll stumble upon the occasional "Paradox Alert." In his book *Psychology and Alchemy,* Carl Jung said, "Only the paradox comes anywhere near to comprehending the fullness of life." You'll discover many paradoxes in your own deep soul explorations. When you find one, stop and look inside yourself. Capture all your divine puzzles. Mull them over. They hold clues to the miracle of life.

Your Journal

You will do lots of deep soul writing, so get a journal in which to capture your "Nourish" statements and "Paradox Alerts" and all kinds of other insights and surprises. Perhaps you'd like to write under the wise, loving eyes of the owl on the cover of *My Soul Pages*, the companion journal to *Writing Down Your Soul.* Whatever journal you choose, dedicate it to this exploration. Almost everyone who goes through the Lotus and the Lily repeats the process and makes a new mandala the following year. Just imagine how exciting it will be to look back at several mandalas and journals and watch how your soul has created life over the years.

Deep Soul Writing

If you've read *Writing Down Your Soul,* you know that deep soul writing is not journaling. It is a unique but easy writing process that moves you quickly out of high-stress beta brain waves into slower, calmer theta brain waves. It is in theta that we have access to true creativity, breakthrough thinking, and divine guidance.

Three things happen when you write at the soul level: You exit the conscious mind. You get in touch with your authentic self, your soul. And you connect with and activate the divine Voice of wisdom within.

There are seven simple steps to transforming your writing practice and get into the theta brain-wave state:

1. Set your intention to connect with your divine Voice.

2. Address the Voice by name. If you have a special name, as many deep soul writers do, use that. If not, simply write, "Dear Voice."

3. Write by hand. It's possible to get into theta while writing on the computer, but looking at a screen pulls most of us back into our conscious mind. If you can, write with a pen so you feel the presence of the Voice in your hand.

4. Activate all five senses:

   - Vision is automatically engaged.

   - The parts of your brain responsible for hearing are firing even if you write in total silence, but if you want to add sound, you can play sacred chants, the *Theta Music* CD (available at my website), or anything else that appeals to you.

   - Touch is automatically engaged.

   - Activate the sense of smell with essential oils, flowers, candles—anything that feels right.

   - Drink pure water after you write to bring your wisdom and insights into your body at the cellular level.

5. Ask lots of open-ended questions. In *Writing Down Your Soul,* there is extensive information on questions that work and questions that don't.

6. Write fast without editing or judging.

7. Be grateful. Say thank you, because you were heard.

One of the amazing discoveries of deep soul writing is that the more time we spend in theta while writing, the more easily we slip into theta throughout the day. A particularly rich opportunity to experience a natural state of theta is during the semidrowsy moments before you are fully awake. Lie still on the pillow and notice what's happening inside. You can also slip into theta while meditating, praying, driving, walking, and taking a shower—a.k.a., the phone booth to God. (Don't laugh. I get so much information in the shower, I had to find waterproof paper.) For more information on deep soul writing and theta, please visit *janetconner.com*.

Foundational Truths

I'm not your teacher. I don't have your answers. My saying this may surprise you, but think about it—how could I, when I don't know your soul's purpose? It's possible that the very thing you are wrestling with—and trying so hard to make go away—is exactly what you're here to unravel. So I don't have your answers, and I don't think anyone else does either.

What I do have are powerful processes that help you activate your own innate spiritual intelligence, communicate at the soul level, and find the answers only you can find. Those are the answers that will change your life.

So who *are* your teachers? Well, for starters, they are you, your soul, and life itself. And then there are our master teachers, the Buddha and Jesus, and the many saints and mystics who reached the highest state of consciousness, called *perfection* or *divine union* or *Christ consciousness*. In the Lotus and the Lily process, we step back in time and stand in their holy footprints for a moment. From there, we can glimpse life as they saw it and allow their profound teachings to enter us—body, mind, and soul.

Here are a few foundational truths of the Lotus and the Lily:

1. The Divine lives in paradox. When you stumble upon a paradox, pay attention. Wrestle with it, and you will learn something about the mysteries of life.

2. Modern science is catching up to what the ancient mystics knew: We are an inseparable whole. Everyone and everything is connected in a verdant sea of information, energy, and potential.

3. When the conscious mind is not operative, information can flow to you from anywhere in the universe.

4. The masters of all traditions perceived the truth and shared it. We are not discovering new truths; we are listening to ancient ones with fresh ears.

5. Answers fill us. Questions open us. We don't want answers; we want bigger questions.

6. Intention and gratitude are two essential inseparable waves. They bless everything they touch.

7. You have the power to create, and you have the power to discreate what you have made.

8. You build an abundant life by creating conditions for receptivity, not by wanting.

9. You don't actually want anything. What you want is the freedom the thing represents.

10. The mandala is the perfect symbol of the union of the human and the Divine. It is a three-dimensional hologram that generates a dynamic relationship with all that is.

11. There are two engines of change: the mandala and full-body spoken prayer. Combine these two consciously and unconsciously every day, and your world will change. It has to. It is the natural order.

12. When one creates a personal universe of joy, all are lifted. As your life becomes sweeter, you kiss the world.

A Few Words on Time

The Lotus and the Lily is laid out over thirty days. Many people go through the process in November and December, so they are ready to have a Soul Day and create a new Intention Mandala on January 1. I teach a live telecourse on the process every November to December for that reason. But you don't have to do it then. Go through this program thirty days before a special date, like a birthday, or any time you feel the urge to create or recreate your world. Whatever date you choose for your Soul Day, be sure to give yourself thirty days to play through the process beforehand, so you can have the whole experience.

For some, thirty days is not enough. They find they want to linger over some of the experiences. If you are going through the Lotus and the Lily with a group, try to keep pace with them. Mark the parts you want to revisit, but give yourself at least a taste of the days the rest of the group is experiencing. That way you can participate in the group discussions. You will find that you learn something in the discussion that you might not have discovered on your own. Group sharing is often the richest part of the entire experience. (Go to *janetconner.com* for information on group-facilitation guides and certification.)

If you are going through the program on your own, progress at your own pace. If you feel you want more than a day for an experience, take more than a day. But please, don't let yourself get stalled on a particular experience trying to finish it "completely" or "perfectly." These rich spiritual practices make up the adventure of a whole lifetime. Each time you return and repeat the process, you'll have a deeper experience. The Lotus and the Lily is not a one-time experience. It is a way of living, a way of walking; it's an ongoing dance of creating life. And as with all dances, we move more easily with practice.

Don't Forget Your Body

You are an embodied soul. That means what your soul experiences, your body experiences. So treat your whole self with tender loving care. Here are a few gifts you can give yourself:

Time. We stay so busy that the truth of our lives can't catch up with us. Set aside thirty minutes or more for the Lotus and the Lily experiences. This gift of time will return to you a thousandfold.

Silence. There is no substitute for silence, because it is in silence that the soul speaks. Turn off the radio; put down your iPod. Make friends with silence.

A media diet. Cut down or eliminate your consumption of fear-filled media. If nothing else, do not watch TV, especially the news, at night. Don't take fear to bed with you.

Prayer and meditation. Spiritual practice is a muscle that strengthens with use. Use those muscles.

Movement. The physical body holds toxins. Throughout this program, you will release many deeply embedded toxic thoughts and beliefs. Help your body release them with yoga, walking, tai chi, massage—something to get your muscles moving.

Water. Drinking pure water helps your body release toxins. Drink a lot of it.

Sleep. Most people report they need more sleep while doing this process. Give yourself the gift of sweet rest. Sleeping more will also give you the benefit of more dreams.

Nurturing. Perhaps that means taking a long walk in nature, staying away from toxic people, walking a labyrinth, or renewing an old friendship with a sacred text. Whatever it is, do it, and notice how you feel.

Personal amnesty. When doing deep soul writing, a woman in Minneapolis was berating herself on the page for yet another failure. The Voice stopped her cold and wrote, "Grant yourself an amnesty. Apply a peace treaty to your heart. You are no longer your own enemy." Take these words to heart. They are a gift for you, too.

You've already given yourself one important gift: you're here. You've heard the call that your soul wants to create life, and you've shown up, ready to begin. Read on—there's magic waiting for you in the mandala.

What Are Mandalas and Why Do We Make Them?

The moon is most happy
When it is full.

And the sun always looks
Like a perfectly minted gold coin
That was just polished
And placed in flight
By God's playful Kiss.

And so many varieties of fruit
Hang plump and round
From branches that seem like a Sculptor's hands.

I see the beautiful curve of a pregnant belly
Shaped by a soul within,
And the Earth itself,
And the planets and the Spheres—

I have gotten the hint:
There is something about circles
The Beloved likes.

—Hafiz, from "Circles," *I Heard God Laughing*,
Translation by Daniel Ladinsky

At the time I made "My Breakthrough Year," on January 1, 2010, with my conditions on a lily at the center of a circle, I didn't label what I'd drawn a "mandala." But thirty days later, when the bankruptcy attorney told me I'd made so much money I was no longer bankrupt, I stood in front of my round drawing, stared at it, and wondered, "What *is* this?" I sensed there had to be something about the shape because I had made several traditional rectangular vision boards in other years, but none of them had been as miraculous as the circular vision board I made in 2006 or this new one in 2010. I searched online and quickly discovered I'd made much more than a round vision board; I'd made a "mandala."

I became hungry to know more about mandalas. I turned to my Voice. "Why," I asked, "does a mandala make such a difference? Show me." Two weeks later, I was awakened in the middle of the night with a picture of my mandala floating in my head. The invisible hands holding it vertically in front of me began to slowly rotate the paper until it was completely horizontal, and I could see only the edge.

When it reached full horizontal position, I saw that it wasn't a piece of paper at all. It was the central slice of a three-dimensional sphere floating in clear black space. The edge of my mandala was the middle line of the sphere, like the equator on earth. Below my mandala were three slender gold threads, like latitude lines. The three gold threads divided the lower half of the sphere into four sections, which I knew were the four weeks of deep work I'd done prior to creating my mandala.

Above my mandala was a cone of golden light pouring onto the lily from a small hole at the top of the sphere. I felt I was seeing confirmation that our conditions are our connection with the Divine. I could see my desires on the periphery of my mandala, but the bulk of the light was falling on the lily that held my conditions.

I stared hard at the sphere, trying to capture every detail in my memory. When I relaxed my attention, I noticed that the golden threads of my sphere were connected to other spheres, which were connected to still others, reaching into infinity. Everything and everyone was connected in clear black space.

I glanced back at my personal sphere because something was moving. The lily petals were coming to life. A stem began to grow down from the petals. Then a couple of leaves sprouted and finally roots spread out from the stem. I could see—literally—how everything in my life had led to, fed, and become my present.

When the vision was complete, I whispered thank you and slipped into a sweet sleep. The next morning, I thanked the Voice for this extraordinary image. On my own, I said, I would never have realized a two-dimensional mandala is really a three-dimensional globe. But I had one question the vision hadn't answered. "How," I wrote, "can I move my mandala— my life and myself—up closer and closer to the Light?" My hand wrote two words in big capital letters: *SAY YES!* I smiled. Of course! I had put my intentions out there; now all I had to do was say yes to everything heaven arranges—yes to guidance; yes to invitations, whether I understand them or not; yes to ideas; yes to intuition; yes to urges; yes to life. I grabbed a piece of paper, wrote *yes!* in huge letters, and taped it to my bedroom wall. Now, when I open my eyes, I see the call to *yes!*

My first call to yes was to learn about mandalas. I began with *Mandala: Journey to the Center* by Bailey Cunningham, founder of the Mandala Project. This book, filled with beautiful pictures that demonstrate the presence of mandalas in every form and aspect of life, was the perfect introduction. Look up: the sky is full of giant mandalas—our earth, the planets, stars, galaxies. Look in: our world is constructed of tiny mandalas—atoms and subatomic particles. Look around: everything is a mandala—your eye, a volcano, snowflakes, sunflowers, spider webs. Our world is a mandala, and everything in it is arranged according to the golden ratio, an ancient Indian formula introduced to the West in the thirteenth century by the brilliant Italian mathematician Fibonacci. Have you heard of Fibonacci numbers? They are an infinite sequence in which each number is the sum of the two before. Begin with zero and I and then 0+1=1, 1+1=2, 2+1=3, 3+2=5, 5+3=8, 8+5=13, 13+8= 21, etc. This sequence is the structure of the Golden Spiral on which all life is based.

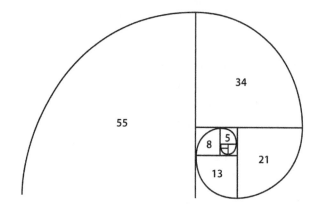

Every living thing follows this sequence. The arrangements of artichoke leaves, pine-cone bracts, sunflower seeds, fern fronds, and tree branches are all living expressions of

Fibonacci numbers and the Golden Spiral. A slice of a nautilus shell displays this geometric form perfectly. Look: life itself is a living, breathing mandala.

From our earliest history, humans have intuited the power and importance of the circle. In her gorgeous *Sacred Geometry Oracle Deck*, Francene Hart explains why: "This most basic of geometric shapes contains within it a doorway to inner realms that has informed and inspired cultures and individuals since the beginnings of humankind." Our first art, a pattern of concentric circles leading to a center point, was pounded into a rock 50,000 years ago by Aborigines in Australia. Our earliest spiritual gathering places were mandalas. Newgrange, a circular mound of earth protecting tombs and passages, was constructed in Ireland in 3200 BCE. Only in the 1960s did an Irish professor discover that it is aligned perfectly with sunrise on the winter solstice. Our most famous and mysterious Neolithic sacred site is Stonehenge. We do not know why it was built or how it was used, but we can't miss that it is a massive stone mandala. All spiritual traditions express the union of the human and the divine with this sacred geometric shape. The Native American medicine wheel, the dome of a mosque, the labyrinth and rose window at Chartres, Celtic crosses, the yin-yang symbol—all are mandalas. But perhaps no culture has perfected the mandala like the Tibetan Buddhists. The intricacy and beauty of a Tibetan sand mandala simply take the breath away.

To paraphrase Hafiz, there is something about circles that *humanity* loves. Why? Because the circle has no beginning and no end. It is the picture of wholeness, of unity, of endless potential. But it's not a static picture. The mandala is alive. As Bailey Cunningham says in *Mandala: Journey to the Center*, the mandala "is both a symbol and *manifestation* of creation" (emphasis added). C. G. Jung was captivated by this manifestation ability. He spent a lifetime exploring the transformative power of the mandala. In his memoir, *Memories, Dreams, Reflections,* Jung described how he began to work with mandalas in 1916:

> I sketched every morning in a notebook a small circular drawing, a mandala, which seemed to correspond to my inner situation at the time. With the help of these drawings, I could observe my psychic transformation from day to day.
>
> Only gradually did I discover what the mandala really is: "Formation, Transformation, Eternal Mind's eternal recreation." And that is the self, the wholeness of the personality, which . . . cannot tolerate self-deceptions.
>
> My mandalas were cryptograms . . . . In them I saw the self—that is, my whole being—actively at work.

Jung wrote several books on the transformative power of the mandala, including *Psychology and Alchemy* and *Mandala Symbolism*. After working with hundreds of clients and their mandalas, Jung observed that the mandala is

> a kind of central point within the psyche, to which everything is related, by which everything is arranged, and which is itself a source of energy. The energy of

the central point is manifested in the almost irresistible compulsion and urge to *become what one is* [Jung's italics]. . . . Although the centre is represented by an innermost point, it is surrounded by a periphery containing everything that belongs to the self—the paired opposites that make up the total personality.

I can attest that there is a driving force to become what my mandala depicts, both the conditions at the center and the desires at the periphery. But it's not something I consciously manage or control. This is a very important point. If someone had told me on January 1, 2010, as I was completing my mandala, that in thirty-one days I would no longer be bankrupt, I'd have said it was impossible. But on the soul level, it was not only possible, but it was also easy and perhaps even inevitable.

Jung explained this miraculous power: "Most mandalas have an intuitive, irrational character and, through their symbolical content, exert a retroactive influence on the unconscious. They therefore possess a 'magical' significance . . . whose possible efficacy was never consciously felt" (*Mandala Symbolism*). This is a great relief. It means that you do not have to, nor should you, have conscious control over everything you put on your mandala. Lao Tzu knows why:

Trying to control the future
is like trying to take the master carpenter's place.
When you handle the master carpenter's tools,
chances are that you'll cut yourself.

—*Tao Te Ching*, verse 74, Translation by Stephen Mitchell

There is something far greater than individual will at work in the mandala. To Jung it appeared as if "the solution, seemingly of its own accord, appears out of nature . . . felt as 'grace'" (*Memories, Dreams, Reflections*).

No one understood this mysterious grace better than Jose and Miriam Arguelles. Their definitive book *Mandala*, long out of print, is my essential mandala resource. Every time I open it, I find something deep to ponder. They begin by explaining the principle of the center, which is the source of the mandala's energy: "The center is the beginning of the Mandala as it is the beginning and origin of all form . . . . The center is symbolic of the eternal potential." Then they explain how we work with that eternal potential:

> Essentially, each human being is a Mandala . . . ; but this Mandala must be developed and created anew for each individual . . . . The Mandala may be regarded as an engine of change, releasing energy to the extent to which the individual using it and concentrating upon it is capable of identifying himself with it. Ultimately, the Mandala leads its user to a visualization and realization of the source of energy within.

I love the term *an engine of change*. It sets my heart singing. But *how* is a mandala an engine of change? For that we need a dose of modern physics. Einstein opened the door when he said, "A human being is part of the whole, called by us 'universe,' a part limited in time and space. He experiences his thoughts and feelings as something separate from the rest—a kind of optical delusion of his consciousness." In *Science and the Akashic Field,* Ervin Laszlo, the great systems theorist, explains,

> [R]esearchers are rediscovering what Einstein realized and ancient cultures have always known: that we are linked by more subtle and encompassing connections . . . . [T]here is not only matter and energy in the universe, but also a more subtle yet real element . . . . In-formation of this kind connects all things in space and time—indeed it connects all things *through* space and time.

But *how* is it all connected? My dream showed everything floating in black space and connected by golden threads. Physicists call that black space the Akashic Field. *Akasha* is an ancient Sanskrit word for the invisible ether in which everything is connected. In 1907, Nikola Tesla, the father of modern communication technology, first postulated that this invisible element exists. In an unpublished paper, he described an "original medium," a force field that becomes matter when energy acts on it.

With modern equipment, scientists can now observe the effects of this original medium—a quantum field of energy that remains after all other forms of energy are removed at absolute zero. They call this primal energy the Quantum Vacuum, Akashic Field, or A-field.

It may be a vacuum, but it sure isn't empty. Laszlo explains that the Akashic Field is superfluid, superdense, frictionless, and positively alive with information. Everything in the universe is not only immersed in the Akashic Field, but everything also sends energy and information back and forth to everything else. This exchange of energy is called quantum entanglement, and it means nothing is separate. Laszlo's startling conclusion is that "all matter is conscious . . . there is no categorical divide between matter and mind" (*Science and the Akashic Field*).

Well, if science can point to the presence of the Akashic Field, then perhaps my best sources of information on the power of the mandala and my vision of the floating sphere were the masters and teachers of the Akashic Record. The Akashic Record is a name for the countless traces of information that have passed through that quantum medium throughout time. Many cultures sensed the presence of this unseen library and gave it a special name; the Hebrew Bible, for example, calls it the Book of Life. This information is so precious that it is protected by highly evolved beings called masters and teachers. With training, you can learn to open your own records. Through the brilliant Akashic Record trainer and reader,

Lauralyn Bunn, I asked the masters and teachers to please explain what I was shown. They said:

> First and foremost, it has geometric information. It is a mathematical representation through symbology of that which is law. The image contains sacred symbols. The gold lines are the grid of information transfer and communication. The black sphere is not a void; it is black as in the law of photography. Black contains all that is yet to be manifest.

Wouldn't Jung have been thrilled to hear this? As much time as he spent studying the effects of mandalas, he did not know that the mandala is a three-dimensional sphere or that it sends and receives information. This 3-D aspect matters because, Laszlo explains, it means that our intentions, our thoughts, our desires—our mandalas—are not only sparks of information that go out into an information-dense universe, but they also go out as three-dimensional holograms. And those holograms have seemingly magical powers. Laszlo admits this image of information as hologram "boggles the mind," but, he says, it makes perfect sense in a quantum, everything-is-connected-to-everything universe. "Through the holograms created in and conveyed by the A-field, things are directly 'in-formed' by the things that are most like them," he says in *Science and the Akashic Field*.

This means that my mandala—my 3-D sphere hologram—resonates only with other holograms holding similar information, like a tuning fork that vibrates only with tuning forks calibrated to the same pitch. And because this resonation happens in a fluid universe, it can happen very, very fast. "[T]hrough torsion waves in the vacuum the A-field links things and events in the universe at staggering speeds—a billion times the velocity of light," said Laszlo (*Science and the Akashic Field*). As I read this, I realized my mandala was not only a hologram, but like a hologram, it also moved. It released energy and received energy. It released information and received information. My mandala was alive. It was a wheel. It spun. It moved.

With that level of information, energy, and speed at play, I guess going from bankrupt to bankful in thirty days wasn't such a miracle after all. Nor are all the other stories I've heard from people in my Lotus and the Lily telecourses, who tell me about the intentions on their Intention Mandalas coming to pass practically before the ink is dry.

In light of the magical properties of our quantum universe, Jung's poetic description of a mandala now makes perfect sense. Quoting Goethe's *Faust*, Jung said the mandala is "Formation, Transformation, Eternal Mind's eternal recreation." I didn't understand this when I first read it, but now I see that when we create our mandala, we *form* it and, in the process, form ourselves. Then, as we live with it and release its powerful intentions and commitments, we are *transformed*, and the whole miraculous adventure happens according to the playful laws of Eternal Mind.

There was a woman in the sixteenth century who understood the laws of this Eternal Mind better than any other woman of her time or perhaps any time. In *Love Poems from God,* Daniel Ladinsky calls St. Teresa of Avila "undoubtedly the most influential female saint in the Western world." These lines from one of her poems, "The Grail," give us a window into her profound understanding of how the world works. It makes you wonder if she saw the universe the way modern science sees the universe.

> They are like shy, young school kids—time and space
> before the woman and the man who are
> intimate with God.
>
> The realized soul can play with this universe
> the way a child can a ball.

After spending a few months in deep exploration of the meaning and magic of the mandala, I've reached a few conclusions. As you move through the Lotus and the Lily and make and live with your own mandala, you will reach your own. But for me, the Intention Mandala is

Organic: It comes from within; no one can make one for you.

Creative: It generates, releases, and receives energy, information, and potential.

Alive: It moves, it spins, it connects, it attracts.

Mysterious: You make it, but you don't consciously know what you are making. You use it, but you can't control it. It creates, but you don't really understand how.

Paradoxical: It comes from you, but it is greater than you.

Ancient: It holds truths our ancestors knew millennia ago.

Mystical: It illustrates and holds the union of your small one with the One.

prepare

In December 2009, I had a burning desire to have a magical year like the one I'd had in 2006. I wanted so much. I wanted to write more books. I wanted a powerful literary agent. I wanted marketing and administrative support. I wanted to teach at renowned spiritual centers. And I wanted prosperity to come home to roost, this time for good.

I began as I begin everything, with a chat with my wise loving Voice. What made 2006 so magical? I asked. The first word that flew through my hand was Advent. *Advent*? I wrote, "I haven't thought about Advent for years. Why do we have to talk about Advent?"

I learned why. Advent was a big deal in my childhood home. In December, we did not get a Christmas tree. We did not go on shopping excursions. We did not decorate the house. Instead, my mother laid on the dining room table a simple pine-branch wreath with three purple candles and one pink. Before dinner, she lit a candle for each of the four weeks of Advent and read a prayer. Advent, she said, was a season of preparation. If you wanted to receive the Light of Christ on Christmas, you had to spend four weeks getting ready.

You can imagine how thrilled we five kids were with Advent. We didn't want to pray. We wanted to sing Christmas carols. We didn't want a bare living room. We wanted a sparkling tree. We wanted to make lists for Santa Claus and eat Christmas cookies. But Mother was in charge, and we were having Advent. There was one small delight. Each day one of us was invited to open a tiny door on a special Advent calendar. Behind it was a picture of a dove or an angel or a Christmas tree—some symbol of the joy to come. Those little pictures spurred our anticipation to even greater heights.

So what did my childhood memory of Advent have to do with creating a magical year? Well, in the course of my conversation about Advent, I realized 2006 was spectacular because I had spent the previous December preparing. I spent long hours in divine dialogue, dissecting how my life was unfolding. I wrote about the past and all its pain. I wrote about what I was learning and all the gifts in my story. I forgave everyone I felt had harmed me. Then I wrote in detail about what I wanted next in my life. After all that preparation, on January 1, 2006, I could write in a firm hand with total confidence: *I am ready.* I am ready for my marketing partner. I am ready for my publisher. I am ready to be in a relationship. I am ready.

The magic wasn't in declaring what I wanted; we've all done that and seen nothing happen. It was in being *ready*. I had given myself a rich Advent. I didn't call it that at the time, but looking back, it's clear that I had prepared my heart, my mind, and my soul to step into the next phase of my life. And because I was totally and completely ready, everything I wanted came effortlessly to me that year.

Preparation is a universal spiritual practice. In every spiritual tradition, a major feast or occasion is preceded by a period of prayerful preparation. Before Yom Kippur, the holiest day in the Jewish calendar, there is a week of preparation. In the Christian tradition, a month of Lenten fasts prepares the soul to celebrate Easter. Muslims fast, pray, and reflect daily for a full month of Ramadan, then end the month with a huge feast and festival of Eid ul-Fitr. In Islam, hajj is the sacred pilgrimage to Mecca, undertaken during five specific days of the Islamic calendar. All Muslims, whether they have actually traveled to Mecca or not, celebrate a great feast of Eid al-Adha when the five-day hajj period ends. The Hindu celebration of Diwali, the festival of lights, goes on for five days, each day honoring an aspect of the harvest; the festival culminates in a celebration of Lakshmi, the goddess of prosperity. Perhaps the longest, oldest, and most famous pilgrimage of preparation is the one that follows the Camino de Santiago (the Way of Saint James), an ancient trail that begins in France and winds across northern Spain to its destination, the Cathedral of Santiago de Compostela (the Cathedral of St. James).

If you want a new life of abundance and joy, your first step is to prepare yourself for it. Give yourself the gift of preparation.

The First Wave: Intention

Begin this week standing still for a moment. Contemplate what you want to experience in this week of preparation and send that desire out into the universe on a wave of intention. At the end of the week, you will stop, look back at what happened, feel gratitude in your heart, and with a sense of celebration, send waves of gratitude and joy back into the universe.

I used to think of these two experiences, intention and gratitude, as two poles—a place to start and a place to end. But then I read about light. Light can be a particle, a specific point, like a pole, but at the same time it's a wave. In this soul adventure, we are becoming aware of our true nature as a spiritual being of light, so we need an image to symbolize how setting intention and expressing gratitude are both places at the opposite ends of a continuum *and* the waves of action that flow between these places.

The movement of a Slinky is a perfect image for the relationship between intention and gratitude. Like the two ends of the Slinky, intention and gratitude are connected and reciprocal. They flow one to the other and back again, and in the process, they move forward together, in the same way the coiling and recoiling of a Slinky moves it down steps. Intention begets gratitude, and gratitude flows from intention. And just as a Slinky won't move unless you give it an initial, intentional push, *you* have to set the waves of intention and gratitude into motion. Nothing happens until you give it that initial intentional push.

If you can get a real Slinky, play with it as you set your intention for this week. If not, hold out your two hands and imagine your virtual Soul Slinky. Lift your left hand gently to send your intention out in a coiled wave. Feel it flowing into your right hand, where it naturally produces an equal wave of gratitude.

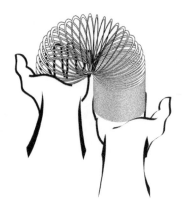

What is your left-hand wave of intention for this opening week of preparation? Not sure? Good. This is a golden opportunity to begin practicing the true creative power of intention. It is not necessary, or even desirable, to have a sharp picture of exactly what you want to experience this week. And really, how could you possibly predict what will happen or what should happen? This week and all of the Lotus and the Lily is a creative experience. When you enter into a creative endeavor with a crystal-clear image of the outcome, you're not entering into a creative endeavor. You're controlling it or managing it or wrestling it to the ground, but you're not allowing it and all its gifts to come to you.

Artists of all kinds are intimate with the paradoxical tension of holding an intention to create while simultaneously releasing control over the result. I heard a rock star laugh when an interviewer asked him how he planned his newest album. The musician said if you know the songs you're going to write, don't bother going to the studio. Fiction writers understand the creative dynamic, too. They are constantly complaining that their characters won't do what they're told.

Now it's your turn. With a gentle wave of your left hand, declare your positive, beautiful, soul-expanding intention for this week of preparation. Then get out of the way. Heaven will take it from here. In seven days, you'll be amazed at all that happened. And you will celebrate by joyfully bouncing springs of gratitude in your right hand.

begin with intention

Intentions shape Light. They set Light into motion.

—Gary Zukav, *The Seat of the Soul*

Everything begins with intention. Whether you are consciously aware of your intentions or not, every move you make is powered by a potent but invisible internal engine—your intentions, thoughts, feelings, and desires. Intention has power. This power doesn't require belief in any dogma, god, or religion. It doesn't require hard work to locate or effort to use. You already use this power every day. You can't help it; it's how you're wired. Teilhard de Chardin, the ground-breaking twentieth-century philosopher, priest, and paleontologist, explained this wiring when he said, "You are not a human being in search of a spiritual experience. You are a spiritual being immersed in a human experience."

You may have heard this famous quote and even repeated it yourself. But have you stopped to consider what he is saying? If you are a spiritual being, that means you are made of the stuff of spirit. What is that? In our simplest understanding, a being of spirit is made of light and energy—intangible substances that flow effortlessly and instantaneously to places we cannot physically reach.

We visualize angels and gods as spiritual forms. But set aside religious imagery for the moment and play with science. Consider what happens when sunlight bursts through a prism.

You can't grasp the exploding rainbow; you can't put it in a box. Yet it is real. And it affects you. For a moment, you are lost in rainbow joy. After that experience with one dollop of light, spend some time with a few Hubble photographs of stars born billions of years ago. You will be stunned by the power and magnificence of light.

Ah, you say, that's the universe, and the universe is stunning. But you are, too. You have to be. You are a part of it. A less-famous quote from Teilhard de Chardin captures your creative power, "The universe as we know it is a joint product of the observer and the observed."

Since de Chardin died in 1955, science has verified his words. In *The Intention Experiment,* Lynne McTaggart summarizes decades of research demonstrating that the outcome of an experiment is influenced by the attention and intention of the experimenters. In a chapter titled "The Human Antenna," she describes evidence that "[d]irected intention appears to manifest itself as both electrical and magnetic energy and to produce an ordered stream of photons . . . [O]ne well-directed thought might be like a laser light . . . ." Scientists can even measure the light coming off the top of your head. So that light in the rainbow and barreling through the universe for a few billion years—that's you, too. How lovely to know that the spiritual axiom that we are light is actually true.

McTaggart's conclusion is thrilling: "Intention appears to be something akin to a tuning fork, causing the tuning forks of other things in the universe to resonate at the same frequency." If this is true in the big labs of science, it must also be true in the small lab of your life. So starting today, use your power as a spiritual being of light to influence your spot in the universe by setting your intention for this thirty-day experiment with the Lotus and the Lily.

You have nothing to fear. You are in good hands. Not mine so much, although I will share with you everything I experienced and learned. But you're in much wiser hands than mine. For the next thirty days you will walk with the masters the Buddha and Jesus, and you will hear the wisdom of Hafiz, Rumi, Meister Eckhart, Lao Tzu, and many other mystics. This process is a grand experiment, indeed, and now is the time to influence your experiment. This is the perfect moment to focus your light and get your tuning fork vibrating. What do you want? Why are you here? What do you hope to experience, learn, create? Spend some time today getting clear about your intention.

Then speak your intention aloud, sending the vibration of your desire out into the world on the waves of your voice. Speech has creative power. In the Bible, creation itself is recorded as a series of spoken commands beginning with "and God said." But it isn't just the First Creator who has this creative voice. "Any word spoken with clear realization and deep concentration has a materializing value," says Paramahansa Yogananda in *Autobiography of a Yogi*. Speak your intention for the Lotus and the Lily today and every day for the next thirty days.

Don't be surprised or concerned if your intention changes as you go. You are going to be dancing with profound teachings, and your soul will move in response. When you feel the urge to change your intention, change it.

But don't skip this important first step. Intention is not only what you do on the first day; it's also what you do on the last day when you create your Intention Mandala. And it won't stop then. As Lynne McTaggart reminds us, "[T]houghts are capable of profoundly affecting all aspects of our lives. As observers and creators, we are constantly remaking our world at every instant."

It is day one, and you have just experienced a double dose of the creative power of intention: you set your intention for the week and conjured up an intention for the whole program. In the process, you have discovered your first nourishment: you are a spiritual being, and one of your great powers is intention.

Reflect

- Why am I here? What motivated me to undertake this process?

- What do I want? What do I hope will happen?

- What are my expectations?

- Can I set an intention but then let go of the outcome? How do I do that?

- What is my intention? Is this my true intention, or do I have another, more hidden one? If everything were stripped away, what would be my true underlying intention?

Write

Dear Voice,

Why did I get this book? Why am I embarking on this program? Where did the urge to do this come from? What do I want? If I'm honest with myself and with you, what is my heart's desire for this whole experience? I believe intention is powerful, so I don't want to be casual about this. Help me clarify why I'm here. And help me let go of telling you how it should look. I'd much rather you were in charge of that. The journey is beginning, and I am excited. Declaring my intention is the first thing we are doing together on the page. So help me, what is my intention?

Explore

- Play with light. Find a prism and stick it in bright sunlight. How does it feel to hold a rainbow in your hand?

- Play at the Hubble site *hubblesite.org/gallery.*

- Play with a tuning fork. Watch how it influences everything around it.

- Allow your intention to make itself known. If it pops to the surface, write it down. If it doesn't, don't worry. Pray, meditate, write, or go for a walk. Or ask for guidance as you fall asleep; then notice your dreams and waking thoughts. Ask for help and allow information to come to you. Don't judge it—just ask and receive. But do not ask another person to help you with your intention. This is your month, your adventure, your life. Your answers are inside of you.

- When a phrase or sentence resonates in your heart, you've got your intention. Write it on a beautiful card or do something special to honor it. Speak your intention, see how it sounds, then say it aloud every day.

Nourish

I am a spiritual being with the power of intention.

Want More?

- Read *The Seat of the Soul* by Gary Zukav.
- Read *The Intention Experiment* by Lynne McTaggart.
- Read *Autobiography of a Yogi* by Paramahansa Yogananda.

Day 2

you're not alone

I can
See angels
Sitting on your ears,

Polishing trumpets,
Replacing lute strings,
Stretching new skins on the drums
And gathering wood for the evening's fire.

They all danced last night
But you did not
Hear them.

—Hafiz, from "I Can See Angels," *The Gift,*
Translation by Daniel Ladinsky

Why do we feel alone? We know intellectually that we can't be. Even the least scientifically inclined has heard enough physics to know that we are made of energy. (Thank you, Albert Einstein, for a formula so simple that even I, who barely scraped through algebra, can understand it.) And if we're all energy, then it isn't much of an intellectual leap to realize we are all connected. So why then, if we understand the way the universe is constructed, do we feel so alone? I do not have an answer for this. It seems to be the human dilemma. We are all one, but on any given morning, we can wake feeling like one lone person chasing answers, one soul seeking peace, one heart seeking hope.

I know I'm not alone, but I can still feel alone. So every day I stand in front of my altar and say again, out loud, what I know to be the truth. I don't say it for heaven. Heaven already knows. I say it for me. I say the words to remind myself that Spirit is with me. My guides are with me. My guardian angel is with me. I know the Archangel Michael is with me. And the Archangel Gabriel? She's with me. She has to be. She is the loving protectress of all writers. I call on her and her copper orange light every time I write.

I know my parents are with me, too. Dad has appeared to me as a cardinal, his favorite bird, for years. He shows up in the tree outside my dining room window at dusk. When I hear his chirps, I stop, say hello, and thank him for watching over me. After Mom died in 2007, I wondered when she'd show up. One evening last winter, Dad peeped his twilight hello. I went to the window and asked, "Where's Laurene?" Immediately his beautiful orange mate flew to the tree. I cried tears of greeting and thanksgiving. Since then, they've always come as a pair. On a long walk recently, I felt lonely and scared and said in a whisper, "Mom, Dad, I need you." I rounded the corner and there they were in an oleander bush at eye level, just eighteen inches away.

I am not alone. And neither are you. But do you know *who* is with you? It could be angels, saints, spirit guides, animal messengers, loved ones, goddesses, fairies. It could be a whole chorus of helpers. In fact, it probably is. Wouldn't life be easier, and a whole lot more fun, if you knew who was with you and how to turn to them for help? There are several things you can do to become more aware of your companions. Start with deep soul writing. Ask who's with you. Ask for a sign—something unmistakable. Then pay attention to what happens. Take nothing for granted—nothing. Angels, I swear, have a wacky sense of humor. Don't assume something small or weird or odd isn't a signal from them. Last fall, for example, a penny miraculously showed up on my teaching table as I was concluding a Writing Down Your Soul workshop in Austin, Texas. I gasped, held it to my heart, and whispered thank you. As we were saying goodbye, a woman told me she'd found the penny on the floor and put it on my table. I thought, oh well, I guess this one wasn't from the angels. When I got home that night, there was a shiny penny smack in the middle of my bedspread. I laughed, "Sorry I ever doubted you!"

Over my crib, my mother hung a painting of a huge guardian angel walking behind a little girl. That painting reminded me every day that my guardian angel was with me. So angels have always felt real to me. But if you don't have a relationship with angels or wonder if they're even real, the book for you is *Angels in My Hair* by Lorna Byrne, who has seen and talked with angels since she was a baby.

An easy way to get a message from the angels is through angel cards. I like all of Doreen Virtue's angel oracle decks, but my favorite is the *Archangel Oracle Cards.* On the anniversary of my ex-husband's death—a date that is always wrenching for our son—I got down on my knees on my prayer rug and begged the cards for a comforting message for Jerry. I breathed on the cards and drew the card called "Hello from Heaven." The card's message from Archangel Azrael said, "Your loved ones in heaven are doing fine. Let go of worries and feel their loving blessings." Once I stopped crying, I called Jerry. He was so, so grateful for the message.

If you'd like to have a personal conversation with the angels, have an angel guidance reading. My favorite angel-guidance reader is Margo Mastromarchi. Any time I'm facing a big decision or need clarification, I schedule a reading with Margo. (Rest assured the angels had plenty of input on this book.) Margo and I occasionally host live conference-call events with the angels. The angels tell Margo the topic. Members of the event submit questions, and through Margo, the angels answer them during the call. Somehow everyone receives exactly the message she needs.

Animals can be messengers, too. In *Writing Down Your Soul,* I tell the story of the osprey who landed in the tree outside my bedroom window the morning I woke knowing I was afraid of my husband. The osprey stayed with me for a year and a half. Every afternoon he'd scream until I'd run into the backyard and show him I was fine. Ospreys have appeared as my protectors ever since.

If I sense an animal is a messenger, I stop and ask it to tell me why it came. I also look up the mystical meaning in the book *Animal Speak* by Ted Andrews or in *Medicine Cards,* an oracle deck by Jamie Sams, David Carson, and illustrator Angela Werneke. The proposal for this book got finished with the help of a woodpecker. The rhythm of her pecking on the wood outside my window motivated me to keep pecking at the computer. In *Animal Speak,* Ted Andrews says the message of a woodpecker is "[T]he foundation is there. It is now safe to follow your own rhythms." I finished the proposal in two days. The moment it was complete, I rushed to the window to thank the woodpecker. She flew off, never to be seen again.

It doesn't matter how you go about becoming aware of your support team. What matters is knowing you're not alone, calling for help, and recognizing the presence of your guides. Get to know and love your divine team. They will be your best friends from now on. And don't forget to say thank you.

Reflect

- Who are my guides? Are angels around me? Animal messengers? Something else? Do I know? If not, what do I want to do to find out?

- How do my guides show up? When have I been aware that I am not alone?

- What messages or comfort have they given me?

- How can I work more closely with my angels and guides?

Write

Dear Voice,

I love this idea of not being alone, but the truth is, I do often feel alone. I can slip so easily into that black space where I feel no one is with me, no one is listening. Then I pick up a pen and start to write, or something else happens, and I sense I'm being guided. I'd like to have that feeling all the time. I'd love to walk this earth knowing I am guided and protected. Help me see that. Know that. Feel that. Who are my guides? How am I guided? Help me tune into them and their guidance so I can be stronger, clearer, more connected all the time. I'd love that.

Explore

- If you have a relationship with your guides and angels, continue to say hello every day. Keep the conversation alive.

- Ask for help. The angels, according to Lorna Byrne and Margo Mastromarchi, love being asked to help. So ask. Ask with vigor. Ask your angels to let you know they are there. Then keep your antennae out. They may communicate with you in some interesting ways.

- If you have oracle cards that you like, use them to ask for information about your guides. If you don't, look at sample decks at metaphysical bookstores, or ask your friends if they can recommend a deck.

- If nothing else, say out loud that you want your guides to show up and let you know they're there. Something will happen. They'll send you some kind of signal. But you have to pay attention and acknowledge the message.

Nourish

I am not alone. I have a loving spiritual support team.

Want More?

- Read *Angels in My Hair* or *Stairways to Heaven* by Lorna Byrne.
- Check out Margo Mastromarchi's website, Oracle of the Dove (*oracleofthedove.com*).

Day 3

you are your own shaman

We can be the curates or curators of our own souls, an idea that implies an inner priesthood and a personal religion. To undertake this restoration of soul means we have to make spirituality a more serious part of everyday life.

—Thomas Moore, *Care of the Soul*

My parents insisted I go to a Catholic college so I wouldn't lose my faith, but by my sophomore year, all my friends and I stopped going to church. Protesting the Vietnam War seemed more meaningful. I made a big mistake, though: I tossed out the proverbial baby with the bathwater. I consciously wanted to toss out the dogma and rules and endless focus on sin, but in the same whoosh, I threw out all the beautiful practices, prayers, mystical symbols, and songs. I threw out every method I knew to connect with the Divine.

It wasn't until I woke one morning, forty and pregnant, that I felt an urge to reconnect. I tried going back to a Catholic church, but it didn't feel right. Then I tried an Episcopalian church. That went pretty well until I helped my three-year-old bless himself as the priest intoned the closing benediction, "In the name of the Father and of the Son and of the Holy Spirit, Amen." In the silence that followed, Jerry turned to me and asked in a loud theatrical whisper, "Where's God the mother?"

That excellent question sent me searching for a feminine deity. When I discovered that not only was God originally worshipped as the Goddess, but she was also served by priest-esses, well, I was tickled pink. The girls were back! But after a couple years, I wondered whether it was really better to have only women and no men in charge of theology and ceremony. Why couldn't we both, women and men, be emissaries to the Divine?

On day three of my first time doing the Lotus and the Lily process, I was having a chat with my wise loving Voice when a phrase popped onto the page: "I am my own priest." I sucked in my breath. The little Catholic girl who still resides under my skin was scandalized. "Whaddya mean, I am my own priest?" I wrote. But of course, the Voice was right. I am, you are, we all are our own priest-priestess-shaman-rabbi-imam. No inter-mediary is required. No intermediary is necessary. Sometimes perhaps, no intermediary is even desired.

Now, I know it's lovely to pray alongside someone who has a profound prayer practice. It is divine to be in the pres-ence of someone holy. It is comforting to hear someone else's words of prayer and hope. But you can connect with the Divine yourself. You can make that connection right now. In your kitchen. At the computer. Lying in bed. In the shower. Driving to work. Folding the laundry. You have direct and immediate access to Spirit. We all do. We just forget.

I find this a relief. Connecting with the Divine is not about finding the right priest or shaman. It's not about finding the right religion, the right prayers, the right ceremonies. It's about standing in the sacred space that you create, calling forward the words that come from your soul. And it's about connecting, deeply and truly connecting, with that which you know to be holy.

That's what we're doing today. We are all becoming our own priests, our own priestesses, our own shamans. We are all stepping into our innate spiritual power and saying to our divine Source, "Here I am. How can we get closer?"

How does that feel? Are you ready to declare that you are your own shaman?

Reflect

- Do I feel I am my own priest/priestess/shaman?
- Does that feel comfortable? Powerful? Good? Or does it feel sacrilegious? Presumptuous? How about ridiculous?
- Do I feel truly, deeply, and intimately connected with my divine Source? If not, what's in the way?

Write

Dear Voice,

I am in a bit of a quandary about this. Yes, you and I talk on the page, and I know it's a connection with something bigger, greater, wiser than me. Sometimes I think that something is God, and sometimes I'm not sure. But does connecting with it elevate me to being my own shaman? Shamans have serious power! I don't feel like I have a whole lot of power to invoke God. That's why I'm doing this program, for heaven's sake. I'm learning, or wanting to learn, to create prayers that work. Yes, I pick up a pen and write to something godlike. I just never connected the dots all the way to "I am my own priest." Let's talk about this. Am I directly connected to you? To the power of God? Does that make me a shaman? What does it really mean to be directly connected with the peace and strength and power of God?

Explore

- Play with this idea of being your own priest/priestess/shaman. Notice how it feels. Is it empowering or uncomfortable? If it is uncomfortable, why is it?
- What does "I am my own shaman" mean to you?
- Ask your guides and angels for guidance on this concept and see what happens.

- Even if you doubt that you can be your own shaman, take it on faith for the moment and allow the possibility to take root inside you. As the month unfolds, you will become more and more comfortable with your innate spiritual intelligence and power. But for today, you don't have to understand or embrace this truth fully. Just try it on for size. Whisper, "I am my own shaman" a few times and see how it sounds. Tomorrow, it will become more real.

Nourish

I am my own shaman. I have direct and immediate access to Spirit.

Want More?

Read the opening chapter in *Care of the Soul* by Thomas Moore.

Day 4

create your own ritual

Ritual maintains the world's holiness. . . . [I]n a life that is animated with ritual there are no insignificant things. . . . The soul might be cared for better through our developing a deep life of ritual rather than through many years of counseling for personal behavior and relationships. We might even have a better time of it in such soul matters as love and emotion if we had more ritual in our lives and less psychological adjustment. We confuse purely temporal, personal, and immediate issues with deeper and enduring concerns of the soul.

The soul needs an intense, full-bodied spiritual life as much as and in the same way that the body needs food.

—Thomas Moore, *Care of the Soul*

You don't have to have experienced Advent, the four-week Christian celebration, or even know what Advent is, to create your own ritual. What's important is to know that humanity from the beginning has relied on ritual to connect with the Divine.

The most stunning book on this topic is *Of Water and the Spirit: Ritual, Magic, and Initiation in the Life of an African Shaman* by Malidoma Patrice Somé. Somé's grandfather was the Dagara tribe's shaman in West Africa. When Somé was four years old, he was kidnapped by Jesuit missionaries and raised in a strict Catholic seminary, where he became a French-speaking scholar. At age twenty, he escaped from the seminary and ran home, but by then he no longer remembered his tribe's rituals or language. The tribal leaders decided the only way he could be integrated back into the tribe was to go through the initiation process thirteen-year-old boys experience. There was just one problem: they weren't certain he would survive. In this astonishing book, Somé offers Western readers an eyewitness account of his initiation and, in the process, demonstrates the power of ritual.

Joseph Campbell's work on mythology and ritual, which he discusses in his book and TV series *The Power of Myth* with interviewer Bill Moyers, clearly demonstrates how cultures around the globe use rituals to connect the human with the Divine. There is a human need to feel connected, to touch something greater, to be fed spiritually by a greater source, and ritual satisfies that need as nothing else.

If you don't like the word *ritual,* and many people don't, substitute a term you do like, perhaps *spiritual practice* or *centering activity*. Regardless of what you call it, ritual has always held center stage in human history. In every culture, ancient to modern, the important events in life—birth, death, marriage, graduation—are marked by a ceremony or ritual of some kind. On a smaller scale, our calendars are full of shared ritualized events, like New Year's Eve or Thanksgiving Day. The way people prepare for the Super Bowl or the World Cup sure looks like ritual to me.

But rituals don't have to be grandiose. Visualize yourself in the morning, making your first cup of coffee. Don't you do it the same way every day, using the same method, the same pot, and your favorite cup? I sure do. Well, guess what, that's a ritual.

The truth is, our lives are a series of small rituals with repeated behaviors, language, beliefs, and expectations. In the Lotus and the Lily, we are taking the concept one step further by stepping consciously into our spiritual intelligence and using that intelligence to create deeply personal, intention-charged rituals. In the process, we restore ritual to its rightful role in life: as a reminder and experience of our dynamic partnership with the Divine.

Throughout this program, you will create personal rituals that will culminate in the design of your own Soul Day. Today, you get to create your first one. Keep it simple. What makes a ritual powerful is that it speaks to you. So design a little ceremony that supports and nurtures your intention for doing the Lotus and the Lily.

To get your ritual-creation juices flowing, here are some components that often appear in rituals. Choose anything that helps you stop for a moment and connect with grace.

- Sacred space or altar
- Statement of intention or purpose for the ritual
- Breath—breathing shifts your awareness and lowers your heart rate
- A call to your guides and angels for protection, guidance, and participation
- Prayers spoken or sung aloud
- Readings from sacred texts or poetry
- Fire—candle lighting or other symbolic action
- Silence or uplifting music
- Sound—bells, rattles, whistles, drums
- Gifts from nature—feathers, rocks, crystals, fruit, flowers, salt
- Holy oils or water—you can bless them yourself
- Hand or body movement
- Gratitude
- Actions that signal the beginning and end of the ritual
- Repetition of the entire ritual or certain actions at regular intervals, like evening or morning

When I began the process that would become the Lotus and the Lily, I went to a craft store to get an Advent-wreath holder like my mother had, but the store didn't have any. I wandered the aisles looking for another idea. Just as I was about to give up, I saw a lone wooden Advent house with twenty-five little gold-trimmed wooden doors. I fell in love.

Every December Ist since then, I get out my December House, set it on a table in the living room, place four votive candles around it, add a tiny brass bell, and finish off my altar with fresh flowers. I cut thirty tiny cards and write thirty things I anticipate being grateful for in the coming year. I put the thirty folded cards in a small crystal bowl in front of the house. Then, every night before dinner, I ring my little brass bell, light a candle, speak my prayer (you'll write yours tomorrow), read one of the cards aloud, and tuck it behind a little door. The whole ceremony takes three minutes, but it leaves me feeling wonderful.

That's my ceremony, but please design your own. It needn't be elaborate. When Brother David Steindl-Rast, author of *Gratefulness: the Heart of Prayer,* lights a candle, that simple act becomes holy: "There is the sound of striking the match, the whiff of smoke after blowing it out, the way the flame flares up and then sinks, almost goes out until a drop of melted wax gives it strength to grow to its proper size and to steady itself. All this and the darkness beyond my small circle of light is prayer. I enter into it as one enters a room."

And don't worry about doing your ritual exactly the same way every day. The key is to show up and repeat something meaningful. Any time you feel a change would add to the power or joy of your ritual, make the change. Nothing is set in stone. You are, after all, your own shaman, and you have the delightful experience of creating your own deeply personal and powerful rituals.

Reflect

- How do I feel about this whole concept of ritual? Does it feel empowering? Weird? Old-fashioned? Silly?

- Do I want to call my ceremony a ritual? If not, what do I want to call it?

- What kind of ritual appeals to me? What do I want in it? When does it fit into my day?

- If I truly were a powerful shaman, what kind of ritual or ceremony would I create to support me as I call in a new life of abundance and joy?

Write

Dear Voice,

I knew in my gut that this program could produce big changes. I just didn't expect it to happen so soon. Help me with this whole idea of ritual. It's a bit foreign to me. What shall I say or do or use? Candles? Music? How about movement? What kind of sacred ceremony can I create to bring me into a state of readiness? I want the result, but I'm not sure how to get there. Talk to me.

Explore

- Create a special space or altar. It doesn't need to include anything elaborate—perhaps just a candle in front of a picture or a precious rock in a bowl.

- Design your ritual. Decide what you want to say or do. Pull together the things you want for your ritual: candles, music, etc.

- Go through your ritual once today. (You'll write the prayer for it tomorrow.)

- Pay attention to how you feel during and after your ritual.

Nourish

I create my own lifting rituals.

Want More?

- Read *Of Water and The Spirit* by Malidoma Patrice Somé, a renowned shaman who performs divinations around the world.

- Search for Joseph Campbell's talks online or at the library.

- Read *Care of the Soul* by Thomas Moore.

write your own prayer

It is impossible for you to come full circle in this way of empowerment without prayer.

It is not enough to want or to intend or to meditate. You must pray. You must talk. You must ask. You must believe. This is partnership. Think of what you are doing as entering into partnership with divine intelligence.

—Gary Zukav, *The Seat of the Soul*

Prayer is necessary. This necessary ingredient is a most interesting phenomenon. In a matter of moments, prayer can alter your vibration, lift your heart, and lighten your load. You know this instinctively from your personal experiences with prayer.

But if, when you began to pray today, someone had attached instruments to your head and heart and body, you would be able see the effects of prayer on printouts and screens. You'd see your heart rate slow down and your brain waves shift from beta to alpha and possibly even theta. You might not see immediate results in your outer world—that is, whatever you are praying for might not manifest right away—but you would see immediate results in your inner world. After years of research in the new area of study called neurotheology, Andrew Newberg, MD, director of the Center for the Integrated Study of Spirituality and the Neurosciences at the University of Pennsylvania and author of *How God Changes Your Brain*, concluded that "different types of meditation and prayer affect different parts of the brain in different ways, and each one appears to have a beneficial effect on our neurological functioning and physical and emotional health."

If you want to explore the impact of prayer on all realms, physical, mental, emotional, and spiritual, read the books of Larry Dossey, MD, starting with the book that woke the world to the efficacy of prayer, *Healing Words.* No one has written more prolifically or more magnificently on the power of prayer.

But even if we didn't have all this scientific input, most of us would still acknowledge that prayer works. Mysteriously, perhaps. Erratically, perhaps. But it works. And that's our focus. We want prayer that works, prayer that creates a beautiful life.

The best prayer, the most powerful prayer, is the one that rises from the wellspring of your soul. Yes, religious traditions have many gorgeous and powerful prayers, but there's something transcendent about writing your own prayer. Coming from your life, your situation, your emotions, your needs, your dreams, your fears, your purpose, and your personal relationship with the Divine, your words have a power that words written by others may not have. This doesn't mean you should relinquish the prayers of your tradition. If you love them, continue to say them and incorporate them into your rituals. But give yourself permission to write your own prayer. It's really quite easy. Just sit down and have a conversation with your Voice. Talk about what's important. Talk about why you're writing this prayer and what you hope it will accomplish. From deep within your soul, ask for the perfect prayer for your daily ritual. Write fast. No thinking, no editing, no judging. Just write.

I started talking with my Voice about how important partnership is to me. The more I wrote, the more I realized that's what the next phase of my life was all about. Once I knew my heart was set on partnership, I asked for my special prayer, and it flowed quickly onto the page:

Today, dear God, I declare my commitment to live in partnership.
  I am rich in partnerships. Michael protects me. Gabriel sends the words.
  Spirit guides me. My spiritual community loves and supports me.
  Now, I step forward into my magical new year as a partner
  calling forth my partners—speaking partners, teaching partners,
  writing partners, publishing partners, publicity and administration
  partners, learning partners and my life partner—
  all the partners I need to live the life I'm here to live.

In return, I commit to be the partner they are looking for—
  present, active, generous, creative, helpful, kind, and grateful,
  and filled with the love of God.
  I share my bounty, and together we do great and meaningful work
  that blesses and heals many, many souls.

Thank you for this past year of learning and growing.
  It is my foundation for my new year of purpose and joy.
  Thank you, God. Thank you, God. Thank you, God.
  I am so blessed. I am so blessed. I am so deeply blessed.

When you speak your own prayer, the words will resonate from your toes to your scalp and your prayer will change your vibration. Plus, I'm pretty sure, your angels will be laughing and applauding and adding their energy so the power of your prayer is multiplied.

Reflect

- What kind of prayers do I say most of the time? Are they prayers of power? Are they prayers of begging? Or something else? Have I even thought about my prayers?

- What kind of prayers do I want to say?

- What's the key idea, the core concept, I want to bring into my prayer?

Write

Dear Voice,

I love this idea of creating my own prayer, a prayer that holds my sacred intention for this life-nourishing process. I want to write a prayer that springs from my soul and reminds me every day that I am a beloved child of a loving Presence. I want to capture the promise of a wonderful future. Help me write it. What are the words?

Explore

- Ask for your prayer on the page, or during the day, or as you're falling asleep.
- Write your prayer.
- Add your prayer to the ritual you designed yesterday.
- Say your prayer once a day for the remainder of this program.
- Think about how you say your prayer. The more of your whole self you put into it, the more powerful it will be. So consider adding water or holy oil, standing, speaking it out loud, and moving when you say it. Keep playing with your prayer and how you say it until you find a way that feels right to you.
- Notice how you feel when you say your prayer and do your ritual.
- Repeat your prayer any time you feel low energy, doubt, or worry. Worry only occurs in the beta brainwave state. Prayer lifts you into theta where you have access to divine connection, insights, new ideas, and peace.

Nourish

I pray.

Want More?

- Read *How God Changes Your Brain* by Andrew Newberg, MD.
- Read *Healing Words* or *Prayer Is Good Medicine* by Larry Dossey, MD.

Day 6

uh-oh!
here comes the opposite!

We should make all spiritual talk
Simple today:

God is trying to sell you something,
But you don't want to buy.

That is what your suffering is:

Your fantastic haggling,
Your manic screaming over the price!

—Hafiz, "Manic Screaming," *I Heard God Laughing,*
Translation by Daniel Ladinsky

Have you noticed that when you say with conviction and joy, "I want ____" (fill in the blank with something good), your heart beats faster, your chin lifts higher, and a smile bursts upon your face? For a moment, your dreams seem so real, so possible. But then the celebration ends when a chorus of naysayers pops up in your head: "Oh, yeah? Who do you think you are? What makes you think you deserve all that?" And when you close your eyes to try to sleep, insidious doubts creep out of their secret holes and poison your dreams. Has that happened to you before?

It happened to me on the first night I began the Lotus and the Lily process. I went to bed excited about calling in a magical new year, but that night I dreamt my house was filled with vermin. There were thousands of bugs crawling over me, my bed, my whole bedroom. When the bugs squeezed under the bedroom door, they were eaten by an army of rats in the hallway. The rats, in turn, were chased by giant rabbits. I woke dripping with sweat. Fear had come calling in a big way, a way I could not ignore.

This fear piece is universal. It happens to everyone as he goes through the Lotus and the Lily. Say "I want," and the opposite invariably shows up. Sometimes it shows up in dreams. Sometimes it appears as stomach-twisting doubts. And sometimes fear shows up in real-life details. It has shown up for me as unexpected bills, dental emergencies, and brand new problems I don't know how to handle. It's as if I said, "I want X," and the universe said, "Oh yeah, Janet, *do* you? Do you really? Show me. Show me that you really want X even when the opposite shows up. Make me believe in you."

If you signed up in your heart, mind, and soul to call in a sweet, abundant, beautiful life, I'm willing to bet your doubts and fears, whatever they are, showed up too. After my nightmare, I went to the page and asked the Voice how to address my fear. I was led to do an oracle-card reading, and the messages of the cards brought me understanding and peace. Look at the "Explore" section of this day's contents for suggestions on how to transmute your doubts and fears.

Don't skip this step. Your fears won't go away because you ignore them. And don't be concerned if they don't melt away the first time you try to dissolve them. Over the next four weeks, you will learn many ways to transmute and even befriend your fears. For today, just recognize the ways that fear shows up and begin to explore how to move through it.

Reflect

- Are doubt and fear poking up their heads? What doubts? What fears?

- How are these doubts and fears showing up? In thoughts, dreams, self-sabotage, emergencies?

- When I say I want something, does the opposite happen? What's that about?

- Do I have negative voices inside of me? What do they say? What do they sound like? If they were people, who would they be?

- How can I transmute those fears and critical voices?

Write

Dear Voice,

This whole opposite thing is so true. Doubt has shown its face. Help! What do I need to know *right now* about my doubts and fears so I can heal them, release them, understand them—maybe even transmute them? Because as long as I've got fear crawling around inside my head, I'm pretty sure I can't create the life I want. Show me how. I'm ready to listen.

Explore

Here are a few ways to support yourself and transmute your fears. Choose any that feel right or find your own method. You are your own shaman and can design your own healing practices.

- Acknowledge your doubts and fears. Talk to them. Get to know them. Identify who they are and what they say. You can call them to come and speak to you on the page (see *Writing Down Your Soul,* pages 222 to 227).

- Write about any appearances of the opposite at length. Keep the channel of divine dialogue wide open. Ask for help and follow your guidance.

- Say the *opposite* of your doubt in your prayers. Throughout my divorce, I prayed, "I am safe and loved" precisely because I did not feel safe or loved. I said this prayer for four years. Then one day, I realized I felt completely safe and completely loved. Find words that calm you when doubt arrives; then repeat and repeat and repeat. Think of it as taking your prayer pill. Nothing is better medicine.

- If you're not sure how to pray, visualize divine love as a bubble of light and see yourself walking into it, saying, "Here I am." This is a lovely way to pray for others. Visualize you and the person you are praying for holding hands and entering the light. Then whisper, "We are here." This is how I prayed for my son when I didn't know what else to do for him.

- Find something comforting to read and read it often. I keep my favorite books of mystical poetry close at hand. Whenever I feel frightened, I take one of the books, hold it to my heart, ask the poet for help, and open it. Somehow, the poem I read is always exactly what I need to hear.

- Avoid fear-filled media. Turn off the TV, especially first thing in the morning and last thing at night. Once you no longer feed your precious consciousness with high-volume, high-fear noise, you'll be amazed at how peaceful you can feel.

- When fear shows up, call on your angels and support team to help you return to a state of peace and faith. The angels are experts at taking fear away.

- Pay attention to your dreams. Look up the meaning of your dreams, or aspects of it, on *dreammoods.com* or other Jungian dream-interpretation site. When you're doing deep soul writing, don't forget to ask your Voice for interpretation and guidance.

- Do a special oracle-card reading. Ask what you need to know to transmute your fears.

- Breathe. When fear comes, stop and breathe, visualizing your body taking in the white and gold light of God with every breath.

- Go for a long walk, but go alone. Your peace is within; talking to others will distract you from that inner conversation.

Nourish

I transmute doubt and fear.

Want More?

Try my "I need help" experiment for yourself. Hold *I Heard God Laughing* (or any other book that you feel deeply connected to) to your heart, ask the poet or author for help, and open the book randomly.

Day 7

stop and savor

Buddhist meditation has two aspects—shamatha and vipashyana. We tend to stress the importance of vipashyana ("looking deeply") because it can bring us insight and liberate us from suffering and afflictions. But the practice of shamatha ("stopping") is fundamental. If we cannot stop, we cannot have insight.

—Thich Nhat Hanh, *The Heart of the Buddha's Teaching*

Congratulations! You have completed an entire week of soul preparation. You are now ready for the next step. But before you go, take a moment to celebrate where you are. Yes, you're hungry for the whole feast, the beautiful new life, but stop and be grateful for the portion you have been served. This is a beautiful time to have a conversation with your Voice. Write about this week of preparation. Explore the insights and discoveries, the surprises and fears. Talk about what was fun and what was difficult. Go over how your perception of your own spiritual intelligence and power has shifted or expanded or changed. Did you discover anything new?

Discover is an interesting word. It is an ancient Latin word that means "to remove the covering." That's what you did this week and what you'll be doing throughout the Lotus and the Lily. You are uncovering the truth that is already alive in your soul. Did you uncover some things that don't look so pretty? Don't judge them. They may be exactly what you need to know or hear or experience right now. Give yourself permission to bless, savor, and even celebrate your week just the way it was.

Don't forget to list all the gifts you received. You may be surprised at what you now consider a gift and by how many showed up. Get used to it. By the time you've finished the Lotus and the Lily, you will have a cornucopia of gifts that will serve you for the rest of your life.

The Second Wave: Gratitude

Do you remember the wave of intention you sent out from your Soul Slinky at the beginning of this week? Look at that intention now and compare it to what actually happened. Any surprises? What has this week taught you about the power of human intention and the wisdom of the Divine? What has it taught you about the power of preparation? What gifts did you receive this week? Take a moment now to stop and breathe and whisper thank you to your guides and angels and the divine ground from which they and you sprang. You are blessed, and you are loved. Say thank you. And send waves of gratitude back into the world. Put that Soul Slinky—real or imaginary—in your hands and with a wave of gratitude from your right hand, celebrate the completion of your first week of the Lotus and the Lily.

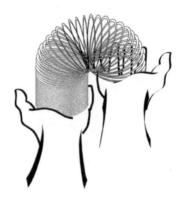

the lotus and the lily

Reflect

- What did I learn about myself and my spiritual powers this week? What truths did I uncover?

- What did I learn about my spiritual partners?

- How different is my intention for this week from what actually happened? What am I learning about setting intentions?

- Do I feel ready to take the next step—looking back at my life?

Write

Dear Voice,

You know, I thought this first week would be a piece of cake. I mean, really, a whole week of preparation? I thought a day or two would be plenty, but then, each day, there was one discovery after another. Now I think I'm just scratching the surface on the power of preparation. Let's go over this week together. I want to understand all the gifts. Let's see, I think the biggest gift was . . .

Explore

- It's a sweet, quiet, easy day. Just stand in a place of gratitude and be grateful.

- Don't skip over this seemingly small step of standing still for a moment and honoring where you are. Learning to stop and savor what is—as it is—is a precious and important way to live.

Nourish

I stop and savor my life.

Want More?

Give yourself a full and complete stop. Here's one way: Go outside and sit. Just sit. Sit still and stare off in space for fifteen minutes. Notice how you feel when you get up.

look back

Last week, you created a personal ritual and prayer to support yourself as you step into the realization of what it means to partner with the Divine to create an abundant life. Don't be concerned if your ritual doesn't feel complete. Just show up every day, and it will naturally evolve until it feels comfortable and leaves you with a sense of connection, peace, and hope.

This week you will look back at your life and extract every drop of learning, blessing, and wisdom you can find. Your life, whether it looks to you like a rose or a thistle, is the manifestation of all the thoughts you've had, the beliefs you've held, the emotions you've felt, the decisions you've made, the problems you've faced, and the sorrows you've endured. And not just the heavy stuff. The life you have right now is also the product of all the sweet moments—all the love and encouragement, hope and prayers—and all the people who believed in you. It's all in there.

So, for the next seven days, you will look into your life as the Buddha would look into a flower: first at the petals, then down into the leaves, stem, and roots, and all the way into the soil to see the food, compost, and nutrients that have fed the flower. Why do this? Because those nutrients are flowing into your life right now, whether you are aware of them or not. And ignoring them, or pretending they're not in there, will just give them more power. You know what that means. It's some sort of dreadful Psych 101 rule: what you ignore will explode in your face, invariably at the wrong place, with the wrong people, and always at the wrong time.

Give all your nutrients, delightful and difficult, your attention this week. Say hello. Get to know them. Get to know them well. Then, as the Lotus and the Lily unfolds, you will have the knowledge and confidence to continue receiving the nutrients you want, turn off the spigot on the ones you don't, and build entire pipelines to find new nourishment.

Don't be afraid of this week. It may have some difficult, sad, even painful moments, but held in the right perspective, it will be a week of discovery and meaning. In *You Are Here*, Thich Nhat Hanh reminds us

> The Buddha said that we should not be afraid of the past; but he did warn us not to lose ourselves in it, either. We should not feed our regret or pain over the past. We do need to study and understand the past, however, because by looking deeply into the past we learn a lot of things that can benefit the present and the future. The past is an object of our study, of our meditation, but the way to study or meditate on it is by remaining anchored in the present moment.

Each of the experiences this week is designed to help you do just that: review the past, unearth its jewels, and return to the present carrying golden building blocks for your future.

The First Wave: Intention

Begin this week with a gentle wave of intention to look back in peace and wonder, to observe how the flower of your life has developed and acknowledge the many gifts you have already received. Send that wave out from your left hand on your Soul Slinky and see what happens.

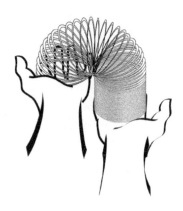

look over your shoulder

There is nothing in your mind
You have not invited in.

There is no event in your life
You in some way
Did not drive a hard bargain for.

—Hafiz, from "Practice This New Birdcall," *The Gift*,
Translation by Daniel Ladinsky

Your focus today and all week is on looking back to uncover
the gifts of your past. At first looking backward may seem
counterintuitive. After all, our goal is to create a beautiful
life going forward. But before you can jump ahead to the joy
of calling in a new life, it's important to take a moment and
look back at the road you've already traveled. Why? Because
you can't build something new, something better, something
more joyful, if you don't understand what you've already created.

The Buddha described this truth when he said, "This is
because that is." Does that sentence leave you scratching your
head? The first time I read it in *You Are Here*, nothing clicked.
Luckily, Thich Nhat Hanh knows that non-Buddhists can
easily miss the depth of the Buddha's essential teaching on
interbeing, so he takes time to explain it. "This is because that
is" means that everything is connected—everything. Whatever

you are experiencing *now* is connected to, generated by, or in some way a response to all that you have *already* created. Furthermore, the life you want to create has to flow from the place you are right now. It can't flow from anywhere else. In a zen-koan-like sentence, Thich Nhat Hanh says, "The present is made up of material called the past and the future, and the past and future are here in what we call the present."

Paradox Alert:
The present is made up of the past and the future, and the past and the future are in the present.

He suggests you look at a plant to understand this paradox. You can see that a plant's growth is affected by the nutrients in the soil, the sunlight penetrating its leaves, and the quality and quantity of water and rain it receives. Well, you are your own flower—or rather, your own field of flowers. So stop where you are right now, stand and plant your feet firmly in your field, turn and look back over your shoulder at your recent past. Or squint even further into the distance. What do you see? What experiences pop up for your attention? What relationships? Jobs? Emotions? Blowups? Sorrows? Joys?

Consider for a moment that none of those experiences is an accident. They are neither good or rotten luck that happened to you. The Tao Te Ching says it plainly: "All of life is a movement toward perfection." All means *all*—the good stuff *and* the bad stuff. The icky situations and upsetting people may be just as important—perhaps more important—to your soul's evolution as the lovely situations and friends. The good news is that all of your experiences are moving you into your wholeness or, in Tao terms, perfection.

So consider the possibility that nothing is happening *to* you. But many, many things are happening *for* you—for your wholeness, for your perfection, for your soul's evolution.

Consider the possibility that on the soul level, not the conscious level, you called these experiences forth. And in some way, each one has helped you move closer to wholeness.

Now, it's normal to look back and shout, "I did not want this, and believe me, I did not ask for it!" Well, maybe you didn't consciously ask for it, but you still called it in. That's the thing with human consciousness, or perhaps we should say human *unconsciousness*. We are magically creative creatures. We are endlessly and always connected with the creative forces of the universe. Every thought has magnetic power. Every feeling percolates out of us to find its match. But here's the problem: it's not just the pretty thoughts and feelings that have power. All thoughts have power. And feelings are even more powerful. Your heart is hundreds of times more magnetically powerful and intelligent than your brain, note Doc Childre and Howard Martin in their book *The HeartMath Solution*.

Worry—an emotion-drenched thought if ever there was one—is particularly powerful. Unfortunately, it invariably attracts more of what you're already worried about. I agree this is a rotten deal, but you can't have the magical creative quality of the joyful, uplifting thoughts and emotions without the magical creative quality of the negative ones. Sorry.

The Buddha's teaching on interbeing is no longer a matter of faith; today it's a matter of science. Every feeling, thought, word, and action that has ever happened leaves a trace on the cosmic field of primordial energy that surrounds and connects us all. In the Bible and the Qur'an, the field is called the Book of Life. In modern parlance, it's called the Akashic Record. In *Science and the Akashic Field*, theorist Ervin Laszlo gives the lay reader the clearest explanation of the Akashic Record I've found: "The informed universe is a world of subtle but constant interconnection, a world where everything informs— acts on and interacts with—everything else." How beautiful that science is finally catching up to what the Buddha knew 2,600 years ago.

To uncover the creative capability of your feelings, thoughts, words, and actions, sit down and have a nice long conversation with your Voice about your history. Talk over what happened in the last year or the last few years. And be sure to talk about how you felt about what happened and what you learned. Then ask some big questions, such as what's the gift? How did this experience help move me toward wholeness? For what possible benefit did my soul call this experience forth?

These can be troubling questions. What if, when you look back, you can see no apparent connection between something you did or thought or felt and what happened? That is often the case in illness, accidents, birth defects, natural disasters, or abuse. And it's certainly the case in the world's horrors of genocide and war.

I do not have a clean, clear answer for why terrible things happen to lovely, innocent people, and I'm not sure anyone else does either. Great spiritual teachers have wrestled with this question for eons. The problem is, I think, that we are trying to draw a short, straight line between a bad cause and a bad effect. But that straight line may not exist. The universe is more complex than that. As Lynne McTaggart, author of the bestselling book *The Field*, explains in her most recent book *The Bond*: "The closer scientists look, the more they discover how dependent on, and finally indivisible from, everything is with everything else." Sounds an awful lot like interbeing, doesn't it?

But just because cause and effect can be an impenetrable mystery, it doesn't mean there aren't gifts to be found. Frances Driscoll is a breathtaking example of how gifts can be found in the most traumatic of experiences. She was brutally raped by a stranger. A rush of poems came pouring out of her in the aftermath. Her book *The Rape Poems* will scorch your eyes, your ears, and your mind. You will never gloss over a news story on rape again. Frances Driscoll doesn't get an answer about why she was raped. She doesn't even try to ask. But her poems have helped thousands of women find a way through their own jungle. Law enforcement and the legal system have turned to these poems to better understand what rape victims experience. Out of her immeasurable pain, Driscoll has given many an unwanted, but suddenly necessary, gift.

If, as you look back, you see a story that feels too painful to explore, be easy on yourself. Remember the Buddha's admonition to look at the past, but not dwell there. And never forget that you are surrounded by love and grace. Don't force or hurt yourself in the name of finding your gifts. Just show up in your heart, ask for help, and your internal divine GPS system will guide you. The doors will open when you are ready. And perhaps, just perhaps, you'll find a little nugget of a gift.

In a *Writing Down Your Soul* course, a young woman took me aside and told me she had endured a childhood of abuse. Before I could think of something to say, she took my hand, looked me in the eye, and thanked me profusely for deep soul writing. With a glowing smile, she said her pages were full of daily messages saying that she was never, ever alone. "I'm so happy," she said and floated out of the room.

Whatever the size or emotional impact of your story, the process is the same: Look back. See your story. Then ask to see the wisdom or blessings or gifts. Dig to unearth the nuggets of knowing. Seek to find all the ways your story has moved you deeper into connection with Source. Look at and honor the steps that you have taken toward a fuller expression of your soul's purpose and wholeness. In other words, find the gifts— all the gifts—that brought you to this moment when you are ready to shift into a new and sweeter life. You can have that new and sweeter life. I absolutely believe that. But not until you extract all the gifts of your story to date.

Reflect

- When I look back over my shoulder, what do I see?
- Are there any recurring patterns?

the lotus and the lily

- Am I willing to consider that my soul actually called forth everything I see?

- How do I feel about the idea that all of life is a movement toward my perfection? Do I buy that? Does it feel right? Possible?

- How would my perception of my life be impacted if I believed that?

Write

Dear Voice,

You know I'd really rather focus on the future, but I get that it's important to look back first. So let's do it. Let's go over the last twelve months for starters. There were some rough spots. I'm willing to look at them, but this whole thing about my soul calling them forth? Ouch. I sure don't like the idea that I called forth _____ or _____. So, let's talk about this. Maybe I did call it to me on some level I don't understand. If my soul somehow sought this situation to help me evolve, well then, I'm willing to dive in and dissect it. Because you know what? I don't want any more of it. I really do want to extract all the gifts—the good, the bad, and the ugly—so I can move on. So let's talk. I'm ready. Let's really talk.

Explore

- This is a tough step for many, so be honest with yourself, but gentle at the same time. I'm not saying gloss over what happened. Quite the opposite. Bring your experiences to the surface and look at them like stones you turn over in your hand, but don't beat yourself up for your choices. If indeed everything is a movement to your wholeness, the experiences that you label bad or stupid or painful may well be the jewels life has provided to help you blossom. So take the gift. Study it. Learn from it. Honor it as a step on your journey to wholeness. But don't get stuck stewing over the past.

- Soul-write about your life's gifts to squeeze out all their juice. This is not a one-time writing experience. Keep the channel open. More and more gifts will emerge this week and throughout the program.

- Call on your guides and angels to support you. You do not have to do this alone.

- If you ask for insights at night, you may have complex, even disturbing dreams. Lie still in the morning and allow the details to come back to you. Pay particular attention to the details in dreams with houses, rooms, or hotels, because buildings are symbols for your inner self, your soul. You can look up the meaning of dreams on Jungian dream-interpretation sites, but your best resource may be deep soul writing. Walk through the dream on the page and ask for insight. You'll be amazed at how well your own soul can interpret your dreams.

- If you're struggling to recognize the gifts in an experience, do an oracle-card reading. Ask what you need to know.

- Don't forget to take care of yourself. Rest, drink lots of water, pray, walk, go to a movement class, meditate, sit outside—do whatever feels right to support yourself.

- Do not fall into the trap of telling your old story to your old friends. It's too easy for them to slip into their expected role and say the standard lines: "Ain't it awful?" or "Wasn't he dreadful?" This will not help you extract any gifts in your experience.

- You'll know you've uncovered some gifts when you find yourself looking differently at what happened and feeling at peace about it, or at least less emotional. (You'll experience the deep release of forgiveness next week. Right now it's enough to notice the gifts.)

- When insights come, say thank you—a big thank you.

Nourish

I look for and find the gifts in my life.

Want More?

- Read *The HearthMath Solution* by Doc Childre and Howard Martin or visit the Institute of HeartMath website (*heartmath.org*).
- Read *Science and the Akashic Field* by Ervin Laszlo.
- Check out Lauralyn Bunn's website, Akashic Pathways (*akashicpathways.com*).
- Read *The Bond* by Lynne McTaggart.
- Read *The Rape Poems* by Frances Driscoll.
- Check out the website Dream Moods (*dreammoods.com*), a Jungian dream-interpretation site.

Day 9

name your movie

For the Celts, the world is always latently and actively spiritual. The depth of this interflow is also apparent in the power of language in the Celtic world. Language itself had power to cause events and to divine events yet to happen. Chants and spells could actually reverse a whole course of negative destiny and bring forth something new and good.

—John O'Donohue, *Anam Cara*

If you look back long enough, and dig into your adventures deeply enough, you'll find a theme, focus, or repeating story. Think of the last year or last few years as a movie with you in the starring role. You know what happens in a good movie. The main character experiences something and has an epiphany that changes his or her life. When a friend asks, "What's that movie about?" you say, "Oh, it's about . . ." You can do that because you have absorbed the theme of the movie. Well, that's what you're looking for today—the theme of your movie.

Once you know that theme, you can give your movie a name that captures the essence, the meaning, the soul purpose of your life's adventure to date. Not sure what that is? Don't be concerned; most of us don't. We get caught up in our daily obligations and rarely, if ever, stop and explore the story we're actually living.

Would you like to know what your movie is about? Its theme? Its title? Then sit down and have a nice long chat with your inner Voice. Talk about what happened in the last year or years. Talk about what didn't happen, too. Look at what you expected to have or learn or do by now. Explore your feelings, struggles, dilemmas, and ahas. In the end, what did you learn? What's your epiphany? As you look back at the scenes in your movie, does an overall theme emerge? How has your character grown and changed? Or gotten stuck? When you have a sense of the major scenes, how your character evolves, and the movie's overall theme, ask the Voice for the title. The name may come quickly and easily. And it may be a surprise.

It was for Jazz Jaeschke. At twenty-three, Jazz began working for a Fortune 500 technology company. Thirty-three years later, her employer presented a severance package that made retirement imminent. Jazz participated in the Lotus and the Lily course a few years later, and when she saw the title of her movie, *Learning to Float,* she laughed. "Since leaving my corporate career," she said, "I'm learning to live free of meeting others' expectations, free of contrived anchors and artificial destinations, I'm learning to float free in the middle of the stream without holding onto safeholds. I don't know how or when this movie ends, but I'm in it, and that's my epiphany."

When I did this exercise a few years ago, I was shocked to see the title on the marquee of the movie I'd been starring in my whole life: *I Don't Know What I Want; Tell Me What You Want.* I was not happy to see this title, but I couldn't deny it. Because I didn't know who I was or what I wanted, I'd spent a lifetime working hard to fulfill other people's desires. Bosses, boyfriends, parents, and teachers had all stepped happily into the vacuum and given me massive amounts of work to do to produce what they wanted. It hurt to admit this. But once I named my old movie, everything changed. The title compelled me to set out immediately to find out what I wanted and to build *my* life. My old movie title was a golden gift.

Jason Howard, another Lotus and the Lily course participant, thought his movie title was a gift, too. *Oh No! Not Again!* is the story of someone who finds amazing things on great adventures, but then is terribly disappointed, grieves, and gets lost in doubt and confusion. But he starts out again, this time more cautious, finds amazing things, and the whole pattern repeats. "I've lived a life of constantly waiting for the other shoe to drop," he told me. "My movie title led me to really explore Einstein's question, is the universe a friendly place? My movie title says no, but that's not the answer I deeply know and want to be true."

Would you like to watch your movie? If it's a tough movie, ask your angels and guides to sit beside you. Watch it through to the end until the credits roll. In the near future, you'll be writing the script for your upcoming starring role in a beautiful new movie, but for now, watch and learn from the one that's playing in the theater of your soul right now.

Reflect

- If I could see my last year or last few years as a movie, what would I see?
- What are the pivotal scenes? Is there an epiphany moment?
- Is there an overarching theme?
- Who had starring roles in my movie?
- What would my movie be called?
- If someone asked me, "What is your movie about?" what would I say?
- How do I feel about my theme, title, main character?
- What am I learning about myself from this whole movie exercise?

Write

Dear Voice,

Well, I've created an interesting movie, haven't I? I love the idea of creating a joyful new one. But let's watch the one

I'm already starring in. Help me see the overall story and how all the scenes fit together. I'm not clear yet about the whole theme. What has this story been about? And the name? What a fun idea. If I could get clear about the name of my old movie, I could get clear about the name of my new movie, couldn't I? Okay, let's talk about this. Tell me anything and everything I need to know about my old movie.

Explore

- Play with this movie idea, but don't stress about it. Just set the intention to know more about your movie and the information will come—on the page perhaps or some other time when you're not paying attention.

- If you're feeling uncertain, ask your dreams to bring you the information you need.

- Ask your guides and angels to hold you close during this process and remind you that you are deeply loved no matter what happened in your old movie.

- If your movie or theme or title makes you sad, honor that feeling. Be kind to yourself. But know that through this process you are creating a new and joyful movie and all is well. Right now, at this moment, all is well. Breathe and remember that.

Nourish

I am the main character in my life's movie.

Want More?

Rewatch a movie that had a big impact on you.

Day 10

spirit winks

If you were God and wanted to communicate with human beings without using a human voice, how would you do it?

You'd perform little miracles, wouldn't you? You'd create little miracles, like coincidences, that cause people to say "What are the odds of this ever happening?"

—SQuire Rushnell, *When God Winks*

Writing Down Your Soul hit bookstores January of 2009. In anticipation, I pinned a huge wall calendar above my desk. At first it looked rather empty. But slowly, as people discovered the book, the squares began to fill with book signings, speaking invitations, workshops, interviews, and telecourses.

I didn't consciously plan a calendar color scheme. The morning I booked my first event, I opened my desk drawer and grabbed a marker. It happened to be black. Joyfully I wrote "Book Signing, Wings Bookstore, St Pete FL" on the square for January 11. Once I posted that one in black, I wrote all my speaking events and workshops in black. I used green to mark the dates of telecourses. Personal dates and travel were written in red. Blue I reserved for surprises—heavenly surprises—miracles, in other words.

Some of my miracles were big. In *Writing Down Your Soul* I tell the story of my son winning a lottery to get into a special free public grade school and the story of my mother suddenly calling to give me the $10,000 I told the Voice I needed. But it's the life insurance miracle that everyone remembers. That one was huge—$322,000 huge.

But most of my heavenly surprises are small—so small, you might not consider them miracles at all. In August 2009, I was invited to speak in Raleigh, North Carolina, but there was no honorarium or travel expense. As I waited for the shuttle van to take me to my hotel, I had a teary conversation with Spirit, "Okay, I'm in Raleigh, and it cost me a pretty penny. Now you have to show me that you are with me and all is well." I stepped into the van, put down my bag, and there at my toe was a penny. When I returned to the airport to fly home, there was a penny under my table in the restaurant. My favorite penny is the one that tinkled at my feet in Wings Bookstore two seconds after I whispered to Archangel Michael, "I need to know you're here."

A penny for me is much more than a penny. It is the way Spirit winks and pats me on the back. I see pennies all the time. One morning, after a fitful night worrying about money, I had to get gas. As I pumped, I silently demanded a sign that I would be okay. The receipt wouldn't print at the pump. "Damn," I muttered, "won't anything go right?" I stomped into the store to pay. There on a white post in front of the door was a dime and two pennies. I whispered "thank you" and took them, but then I added, "You know, two more cents would make fourteen. Fourteen cents would be really nice." I walked back to my car. There were two pennies on the ground in front of my driver's door.

When I got home, I put those coins in a little blue bowl on my "evidence shelf." Whenever I put coins or other heavenly surprises in that bowl, I mark my wall calendar with a blue dot. I love looking at all the events on my calendar in bold black ink, but the real joys are the blue dots. Those blue dots remind me that on that day, my spirit guides winked and said, "We're right here with you, darling." Those are the moments that carry me.

When and how did heaven show up for you this year? Do you have a private language between you and your guides? Does Spirit send you pep talks through coins? Birds? Books? Synchronicities? How about smells or songs on the radio? Or the results of Internet searches? I think the angels are having a grand time on the Internet. I can't count the number of readers who've told me they were searching for something else on the Internet when my books popped up.

If you haven't been paying attention to your messages and Spirit winks, that's okay. Resolve to pay attention from now on. Ask your angels and guides to show up and make it clear they're with you. Then, when you receive a heavenly wink, mark your calendar—in color. A year from now, you, too, will sit and smile and laugh, and maybe even cry, as you look at all the beautiful blue (or gold or purple) days when Spirit and your guides said, "Hello, Beloved, we're right here. We've got your back."

Reflect

- Does Spirit wink at me? How?
- How did I feel when heaven winked? What did I do? Did I acknowledge the gift?
- What kinds of messages would I like to get?
- Have I asked for those messages? What happened?
- If I haven't asked, why haven't I?

Write

Dear Voice,

How fun to think about you and my spirit team winking at me, patting me on the back, letting me know you are with me. I love that. Let's talk about all the ways you've been showing up. If I haven't been paying attention, I apologize. I will from now on. Tell you what, send me a little sign this week and make sure I know it came from you. That can be our secret language from now on. I promise to pay attention.

Explore

- Pay attention to how Spirit shows up to love and support you.
- Ask your guides to send winks and little messages and make it clear they come from above.
- Collect all the signs that you are being guided.

Nourish

I receive messages from Spirit and my guides all the time.

Want More?

Read *When God Winks* by SQuire Rushnell.

Day 11

thought worms be gone!

Go to the Buddha, sit with him, and show him your pain. He will look at you with loving kindness, compassion, and mindfulness, and show you ways to embrace your suffering and look deeply in to it. With understanding and compassion, you will be able to heal the wounds in your heart, and in the world. The Buddha called suffering a Holy Truth, because our suffering has the capacity of showing us the path to liberation.

—Thich Nhat Hanh, *The Heart of the Buddha's Teaching*

Have you noticed that all this looking back, although it's cleansing and clearing and lovely in so many ways, seems to dredge up a lot of rotten old blocks and fears? Are you sick of it? Are you ready to shout once and for all, "That's it. I'm done with you! Get out of here!"

Everyone has old sore spots and relentless fears. Mine is worrying about money. In therapy years ago, I tracked the source of this insidious fear back to my sophomore year in high school when my mother said I couldn't have new shoes. I stared at her across the kitchen table. "But, Mom, look at these shoes. They're falling apart." "I know, dear," she sighed, "I'm sorry, but we can't afford to buy you new shoes." This was a new experience. As a child, I got a new coat every spring and every winter whether I wanted one or not. Now, I couldn't get something I actually needed, a lousy pair of shoes.

During my first Lotus and Lily experience, I did more deep soul writing about my money fears. On the page, I discovered that the kitchen-table shoe scene was *not* the moment they got inside me. Instead, the fears were planted when I was inside my mother's womb. Mom, Dad, my four-year-old brother, and my three-year-old sister were living in a tiny, four-room apartment in Chicago. It was tough to find work after the war, and Dad was not making enough money. As I wrote, I realized that my mother had been worried sick the entire time she carried me. Her panicky thoughts—*We don't have enough money. We don't have enough room. What am I going to do?*—gelled into a parasitic thought worm and passed through the placenta into my brand new spirit, where it festered ever since. At sixty-one, I was ready to yank that thought worm out of my head.

I had a conversation with my Voice about my thought worm. I said, "I'm ready to release it." But instead of instructions, this question came: "What did you learn from it?"

I hadn't considered that. I was viewing my thought worm as bad, something to kill. I turned to the thought worm and asked it to speak. It told me that it had given me many gifts. Fear had driven me to excel in school, earn two degrees, and always make a living. It had taught me to save money and propelled me to take risks on jobs I didn't feel qualified to do. My worm had spurred me to have a powerful work ethic. I was surprised at how much I had received from my mother's fear about money. I thanked the worm, and I thanked my mother for sharing it with me.

But then I turned back to the Voice and said, "All right, I'm ready. How do I release my thought worm?" This is the prayer we developed.

Dear God, I am ready to release my thought worm "There isn't enough money." It has completed its mission and delivered its gifts. I no longer need it, and I no longer want it inside me. It is no longer true for me. What is true is that there is, was, and always will be plenty of money. I now ask that the thought worm "There isn't enough money" be lifted out of me and sent on its way for its own spiritual evolution and for the highest good and mutual benefit of everyone concerned. Thank you, worm. I am free. Thank you, Mother. I am free. Thank you, God. I am free.

As I said the prayer, I visualized my mother's placental fear "There isn't enough money," as a parasitic worm crawling up my spine, along my chakras, and out the top of my head, to be taken by Spirit to be transformed. I said my thought-worm release prayer out loud three times a day for one week. I felt lighter. Freer. Happier. More hopeful and peaceful. And richer.

Want to try? Do some deep soul writing to identify the parasitic thought worm that's been living in your consciousness for years. (You may have several, but address one at a time.) Once you name a worm, pray it out. You are welcome to use my prayer—just substitute your own thought-worm phrase. Or better still, write your own prayer. It's not the words themselves that carry the releasing power; it's your crisp, clear intention to extricate your thought worm from your consciousness and give it to the Divine. If you need help, use Hafiz's suggestion:

Write all that worries you on a piece of parchment;

Offer it to God.

Even from the distance of a millennium

I can lean the flame in my heart

Into your life

And turn

All that frightens you

Into holy

Incense

Ash.

—Hafiz, from "Troubled," *The Gift,*
Translation by Daniel Ladinsky

Are you noticing how all the days in this week connect? It's as if one experience like your movie title feeds the next, your Spirit winks, and the next, your thought worms. This is what happened to Alice Manning in San Francisco. Her movie title was *The Girl Who Could Never Believe She Was Good.*

Realizing that was my movie title, after so many years of therapy and healing work was a blow. I'm still reeling from it. My movie title is also my thought worm. It hurts, and yet it is a gift to see the ongoing ravening of that astonishingly robust thought worm. It isn't completely gone, but I promised myself I'd stop feeding it. I also had a Spirit wink. The other morning I was saying my daily Lotus and Lily ritual prayer and was inspired to tweak it to include the word "conflagration" and to add "may we all be consumed in the Light." Immediately upon finishing my prayer, I picked up today's exercise and read Hafiz's poem, in which he says "I can lean the flame in my heart into your life and turn all that frightens you into holy incense ash." I about fell out of my chair.

Reflect

- What do I think of this whole thought-worm idea?
- What are my thought worms? How long have they been there?
- Do I know where they came from? Am I willing to explore their source? Does it matter?
- Have I been feeding my thought worms? How?
- Can I imagine a life without these old negative thoughts? What would it be like?
- Do I think I can just pray them away? Am I willing to try?

Write

Dear Voice,

Wow, thought worms. What an idea. I get it. I've got a couple of parasitic thoughts living deep in my being, and I am absolutely ready to dig them out and give them away. So let's talk about this. What is my number one thought worm? I know. It's ____. Okay, now, let's get rid of it. Shall I say Janet's prayer or write another? How shall we work together to expel my worm?

Explore

- Get clear about your thought worms. If you're not sure, ask on the page or ask for insights before sleep. Pay attention to your dreams. They might be surprising, even shocking.

- Ask your guides and angels for support and guidance.

- Take my thought-worm release prayer or write your own.

- Say your thought-worm release prayer every day for a week or as long as you feel guided. Visualize your thought worm coming out of the top of your head as you say it. Pay attention to what happens and how you feel.

- If a thought worm doesn't want to leave, don't panic and don't fight it. Talk to it. Invite it to a deep-soul-writing conversation. Ask it why it's here and what it wants to teach you. Tell it you appreciate its lesson, but now you are finished with that part of your story and it is free to go.

- If your thought worm shows up again—and they do like to sneak back in; it's the "uh-oh, here comes the opposite" principle—notice it, recognize it, remind it that you've already acknowledged its gifts, then pray it on its way.

Nourish

I release my thought worms.

Want More?

Read the opening chapter in *The Heart of the Buddha's Teaching* by Thich Nhat Hanh.

Day 12

don't go back to sleep!

The breeze at dawn has secrets to tell you.
Don't go back to sleep.
You must ask for what you really want.
Don't go back to sleep.
People are going back and forth across the doorsill
where the two worlds touch.
The door is round and open.
Don't go back to sleep.

—Rumi, from *The Essential Rumi*,
Translation by Coleman Barks

"The door is round and open." How's that for a simple truth? But what do we do? Why, we fall crashing into the sleep of an unconscious life and then whine and complain about how hard life is, how unfulfilled we feel—how disconnected, how lonely, how sad. We complain that we don't get what we want, what we so clearly deserve. But is that the door's fault? No. The door to the inner world is open. The door to the soul is round. The door to the inside journey, the door to real human and spiritual connection, the door to peace, the door to fulfillment, the door to joy is open. So who's got a problem here? Why, we do.

As you look back this week, ask yourself: When was I wide awake this month, this year, this decade? When was I aware of what was happening? When was I in touch with my soul's purpose? When was I connected with my best self, my soul, my full expression? When did I walk through that door and touch what's real, what's true, what's holy?

Then ask yourself: When did I look the other way? When did I stay so busy that I became oblivious to what I was feeling? When did I avoid real conversations with myself, my soul, my Source? When did I numb myself rather than feel what I'm feeling? How did I numb myself? With food, drink, television, work, sex, media, medication, drugs? When did I pretend I didn't feel the pain? When did I pretend I didn't see the dishonesty—mine or others'? When did I pretend that everything was okay when everything was not okay? When, in Rumi's words, did I go back to sleep—back to the old habits, the old fears, the old assumptions, the old numbness?

Look at your past for a pattern of waking and sleeping. When did you get your arms around what keeps you alive? And when did you go back to sleepwalking through life? When you can clearly see and recognize these two very different conditions, you'll know something *big* about yourself. You'll know something that could make a profound difference in creating the life you want. Do you want a beautiful, abundant, magical life? You can have one, but magic comes only to those awake enough to see it and use it.

When Jason Howard of Oxford, Massachusetts, looked at his patterns during a Lotus and the Lily workshop, he made a big discovery.

Becoming aware of what keeps me awake or asleep has been powerful. Now that I'm aware of my triggers, I can intentionally cultivate a feeling of wakefulness even in the midst of circumstances that used to put me to sleep. And when I'm awake, blessings seem to keep pouring in, and I can even appreciate the difficulties and rise above them. Now I let my instinct for being awake and alive guide me rather than preconceived "shoulds."

Reflect

- What are my sleep triggers? What situations or people make me want to go back to sleep?
- What does it feel like to be asleep?
- Are there levels of sleeping?
- What kinds of things do I do to stay asleep?
- What were my most awake moments? What situations or people make my soul sing?
- How does it feel to be truly awake?
- What kinds of things do I do to stay awake?
- How awake do I want to be?
- How am I going to stay awake? What am I going to start doing, and what am I going to stop doing?
- Are those changes going to impact anyone? Am I going to stay awake anyway?

Write

Dear Voice,

Oh boy, this is big. I can see it. It's important for me to know when I am awake and when I am going back to sleep. I know what I do when I'm avoiding. I hate to admit it, but when I want to go back to sleep, I ____ and I ____ and, sometimes I ____. I don't want to live like that. I want to be awake, alive, alert. I want to be looking through that big wide open door at what I am truly capable of being—my whole, authentic, holy self. So no more sleeping. Help me understand what makes me slip back under the covers of unconsciousness. If I understand it, I can recognize it and stop.

Explore

- Look at when you are fully awake, when you are going through the motions, and when you are fast asleep.

What is this list telling you? Is there a lifelong pattern?

- Identify how you numb yourself. How effective are your numbing habits? Do they mask the pain? What else do they mask? Brené Brown has delved deeply into the sources and ramifications of vulnerability and shame. In *The Gifts of Imperfection*, she says, "We cannot selectively numb emotions. When we numb the painful emotions, we also numb the positive emotions." So much for numbing.

- Once you know your triggers and response pattern, resolve to pay attention to those triggers, recognize them, stop yourself from responding as usual, and instead respond differently.

- Explore how you keep yourself awake. What works? What doesn't? How can you have more of what keeps you wide awake in your life?

Nourish

I choose to not go back to sleep.

Want More?

- The mystical poets will keep you wide awake. Here are a few of the books that are my best friends: *I Heard God Laughing*, *The Gift*, *The Subject Tonight Is Love*, and *Love Poems from God*, all by Daniel Ladinsky; *The House of Belonging* by David Whyte; and *Meditations with Meister Eckhart* by Matthew Fox.

- Read *The Gifts of Imperfection* by Brené Brown, PhD.

Day 13

your grandself

No separation between God and humans. When Jesus talks about this Oneness, he is not speaking in an Eastern sense about an equivalency of being, such that I am in and of myself divine. What he more has in mind is a complete, mutual indwelling: I am in God, God is in you, you are in God, we are in each other. His most beautiful symbol for this is in the teaching in John 15 where he says, "I am the vine, you are the branches. Abide in me as I in you."

—Cynthia Bourgeault, *The Wisdom Jesus*

You are almost finished sifting through the sands of the past and uncovering all the gifts buried there. It's been an interesting week, hasn't it? Some days may not have been so much fun. The gifts of our lives don't always come in foil-wrapped packages with golden bows. Sometimes the most important gifts come in the guise of defeat, rejection, loss, pain, or suffering. At the time, we don't consider that crumpled box to be a gift, but that doesn't mean it isn't. It may be the window your soul peeks through to see the road that leads to your soul's full, rich expression. Listen to Alexander Solzhenitsyn on his long imprisonment in a Siberian gulag:

> [I]t was only when I lay there on rotting prison straw that I sensed within myself the first stirrings of good. Gradually it was disclosed to me that the line separating good and evil passes not through states, nor between classes,

nor between political parties either—but right through every human heart—and through all human hearts. This line shifts. Inside us, it oscillates with the years. . . .

And that is why I turn back to the years of my imprisonment and say, sometimes to the astonishment of those about me: "Bless you, prison!" . . .

I nourished my soul there, and I say without hesitation: "Bless you, prison, for having been in my life!"
(*The Gulag Archipelago*, 1918–1956)

Bless you prison? Bless you prison! That's not a man speaking. That's a soul. That's a soul pushing a dark door open, feeling the Light, and taking the first steps down a path that will inspire millions. His words give us a flash of Solzhenitsyn's wise soul-self waking up. In those unbelievable words, we can see his small spirit blinking in the light as it senses its potential to express big Spirit here on earth.

I like to call that appearance of the soul-self your Grand-Self. Just as the honorific Grandmother captures a higher, wiser expression of the motherly qualities of love and grace, and Grandfather resonates with a higher expression of the fatherly qualities of wisdom and protection, GrandSelf resonates with the higher expression of the soul. It is your God-self, your divine self, showing up.

As we complete our second week, look back one last time and notice when your GrandSelf showed up. When did your spirit burst forth with wisdom and grace you didn't even know was within you? When did the ideas in your head surprise you? When did the words in your mouth bless you? When did the sentences on the page take your breath away? When was your heart so radiant that you thought you might float? When were people magnetically attracted to you? When were you at peace, not just still, but experiencing real, vibrant, deep peace—the peace that "passes all understanding"?

Soon you will be creating a veritable playground for your GrandSelf to show up in a big way every day. But your Grand-Self has been with you all along. Stop for a moment and remember when your GrandSelf tapped you on the shoulder and said, "Hello, Beloved! I'm here!"

Reflect

- Do I think I have a GrandSelf, a God-self, a divine self?
- When has my GrandSelf shown up?
- Is my GrandSelf my soul?
- What does my GrandSelf feel like, look like, sound like?
- Does my GrandSelf startle me sometimes?
- What would my life look like if my GrandSelf directed it?
- Do I want to be my GrandSelf more often? How about all the time?

Write

Dear Voice,

What an idea! My GrandSelf. At first I thought, "What?" But looking back, I have had some odd moments when I surprised myself with my generosity, wisdom, and insights. Let's go back over those. Let's see. How about when _____. And _____. Yes, in those moments it did feel like the Divine was moving through me. How can I have more of that?

Explore

- If you want to get to know your GrandSelf better, ask your angels and guides to work with you to keep you aware of the ever-present option to be that Self. Ask them to remind you, nudge you, show you the way.

- When your GrandSelf shows up, acknowledge it. Honor it. Celebrate it. Smile and bless your Self for showing up.

- Invite your GrandSelf to show up more often. Ask Spirit to move in and through you, to bless the world around you.

Nourish

I am a spark of the Divine.

Want More?

Read part one, "The Teachings of Jesus," in *The Wisdom Jesus* by Cynthia Bourgeault.

Day 14

say thank you

If the only prayer you ever say in your entire life is thank you, it will be enough.

—Meister Eckhart

Today we complete our week of looking back. You began this week by sending out a wave of intention to find, recognize, and receive the gifts of the past. Complete the week by sending out the second wave of gratitude.

Do you remember your mother telling you to say thank you when someone gave you something? Your wild-child eyes were pasted to the shiny new thing, and your hands itched to grab it, but your mother's voice would slice through the air, "Say thank you." And you did. You mumbled it, perhaps, without any real conviction, but the words would come out. And when they did, your hands could touch the new and wondrous thing.

Then there were also those other times when your weird aunt with the icky kisses, suffocating smell, and strange presents would gave you something you didn't want. But still your mother would command, "Say thank you." And say thank you, you did. Then the strange thing was yours, too.

By the time you were four, you knew the world ran on please and thank you. If you want something, say please. Before you take it, say thank you.

So let's be four again. Let's look at all the gifts you uncovered this week. All of them. Even the "But I don't want this!"

strange gifts. Reflect on the gifts of the past and jot them down until you have a nice long list called "My Look-Back Gifts."

Sit with your list and say, "Thank you. Thank you for the luscious things—the jobs, the invitations, the surprises, the synchronicities, all the lovely people who said yes. And thank you for the sorrows, the frustrations, the dead ends, the rejections, the people who said no." Say thank you for all of it—the whole story, the whole adventure. Why? Because it is your story. It is the expression of your soul on earth. It is why you're here, why you came. It is what your soul wants to experience, learn, know, become. Rumi understood this:

If God said,
"Rumi, pay homage to everything
that has helped you
enter my
arms,"

there would not be one experience of my life,
not one thought, not one feeling,
not any act, I
would not
bow
to.

—Rumi, "Rumi, Pay Homage," *Love Poems from God,*
Translation by Daniel Ladinsky

Soon, you'll be saying please to call in the beautiful gifts of your future, but for today, say thank you for how your story has unfolded.

Paradox Alert:
You may feel the greatest gratitude
for your most difficult gifts.

Reflect

- What are the top ten things I'm thankful for?

- Are they all happy-happy things? Are there any happy-sad or even sad-sad things? Any surprises on my thank-you list?

- Can I, like Rumi, bow to things that hurt? If not, is that because I haven't uncovered the gift inside?

- What is blocking me from seeing the gifts and saying thank you?

- Am I conscious of divine presence in my life?

- Do I say thank you enough? What can I do so I say thank you more often?

Write

Dear Voice,

Can I say thank you for the whole thing? Am I ready to say thank you and mean it? You know there are some experiences I haven't been exactly grateful for. Can I get to a place of gratefulness? What's missing? What's stopping me? Why am I not ready to acknowledge that you are my divine partner in and through all of it? What thought or belief or feeling am I holding that blocks me from seeing that all of life is a movement toward my wholeness?

Explore

- Make a thank-you list.

- Say thank you for everything on the list.

- Bow to the things that hurt. Don't worry if there are people and stories you are not ready to bow to. You will become ready next week.

Nourish

I say thank you for all.

Want More?

Read *Meditations with Meister Eckhart* by Matthew Fox.

The Second Wave: Gratitude

Think back to your intention for this week and reflect on all that happened. It isn't exactly what you anticipated, is it? That's good. That's your soul stepping in and orchestrating more than you could humanly plan. Get used to it. You are learning how to create in concert with the Divine. It's a delicious way to live.

Do you feel waves of gratitude—even, or especially, for the harder experiences—rising from your heart? Then send waves of gratitude from your Soul Slinky out into the universe as you whisper, "I am loved. I am protected. I am blessed. Thank you, angels. Thank you, guides. And thank you, Divine One. I am deeply, deeply blessed."

Week 3

create space

It's been quite an adventure, hasn't it? The first week, you prepared by setting your intention, strengthening your relationship with your angels and guides, awakening your inner shaman, and creating your own ritual and prayer. Then last week, you looked back and uncovered an enormous pile of rich, if sometimes surprising, gifts buried in the sands of your life. Perhaps that part wasn't always fun, but it was important. Now, in week three, you are ready to plunge into the richest spiritual adventure of all: creating space for the new by releasing and forgiving the old.

Why is it important to create space? Because you must be empty to make room for the new.

There,

> where clinging to things ends,
> is where God begins to be.

If a cask is to contain wine,

> you must first pour out the water.
> The cask must be bare and empty.

Therefore,
if you wish to received divine joy and God,

> first pour out your clinging to things.

Everything that is to receive

> must and ought to be

>> empty

—Meister Eckhart, from *Meditations with Meister Eckhart*,
by Matthew Fox

Forgiveness is the most important, most essential, and most freeing spiritual practice. But truth be told, we don't want to do it. We don't relish the idea of releasing old anger or forgiving those who hurt us. We've hung on to our wounds for so long that, in a strange way, they've become old friends.

But here's the problem, those old friends are taking up room—physical room—in your body, your memory, your consciousness, your cells, and even your brain in the form of well-etched neural pathways. Those friends are squatting on precious mental, emotional, and physical real estate that could be made available for something new. Something fresh. Something miraculous. And that's what we want. That's what we're here for. That fresh new life of wisdom, grace, and joy is possible. But first, we have to create space for her. "Another world is not only possible, she is on her way. On a quiet day, I can hear her breathing," writes Arundhati Roy in her book *War Talk*.

the lotus and the lily

Listen. Do you hear your new world coming? She's getting closer. In just two more weeks, you will infuse your Intention Mandala with the images of your new world and begin the daily practice of bringing her to life. Creating space is the next and most important step in that process.

The First Wave: Intention

Begin this week as you begin everything: by sending out waves of intention. What is your intention for this week of creating space? Perhaps at the starting gate, you're not certain. Forgiveness right now may feel too big or too indigestible. Standing where you are right now, you aren't sure how this week will unfold, or how you'll feel, or if you can even do it. That's okay. Just set your intention to create space for your beautiful life. See that—beautiful, fresh, open space. Then take a deep breath. Exhale. And listen.

Day 15

universe cash

Forgiveness
Is the cash you need.

All the other kinds of silver really buy
Just strange things.

Forgiveness is part of the treasure you need
To craft your falcon wings
And return

To your true realm of
Divine freedom.

— Hafiz, from "Forgiveness Is the Cash," *The Gift*,
Translation by Daniel Ladinsky

Forgiveness is miraculous. I know. I lived it. In 2001, I wrote a prayer-poem called "Finally Forgive," in which, after years' worth of kicking and screaming, I finally forgave my ex-husband for all the pain I'd been blaming him for causing during our divorce. Within hours of writing it, my ex handed me a check for half our son's last dental bill. This was amazing. For four years, he'd refused to pay a cent of our son's medical expenses, and I'd given up all hope of reimbursement.

But that check was just a tiny hint of the miracle to come. When my ex-husband died two years later, I discovered that he had fought with his life-insurance company to get his policy reinstated, increased the amount, and named me—me!—beneficiary. When I held that check for $322,000, I knew I was holding tangible proof of the power of forgiveness.

The first time I read "Finally Forgive" in public, a woman called three days later. She said:

> You're not going to believe what just happened! When you started reading, I thought, "I'll listen, but I'm too angry to forgive." But then, something happened. The words entered my heart, and something let go inside me. I felt peace about my ex-husband and about my life for the first time in years. I thought *that* was a miracle. But he just called! He deeded the house over to me! Out of the blue. I never dreamt anything like this could happen!

Every time I read "Finally Forgive," I get a call like this one. It always begins, "You're not going to believe what just happened." Oh yes, I am. Because I know that forgiveness—complete, visceral, down-to-your-toes forgiveness—is nothing less than a miracle. It creates wide-open spaces for new feelings, new choices, new actions—on your part and, yes, even on the part of the other. Spirit flies into those new empty spaces, and miracles truly do abound.

Paradox Alert:
If you forgive with the intention of manipulating another person's behavior, it's not forgiveness.

You will read and experience "Finally Forgive" at the end of the week, but please don't jump ahead. Releasing and forgiving are big, and it is wise to take them in incremental steps.

Does the word *forgive* sound heavy? Difficult? Something for saints? The word in Greek simply means "untie the knot."

That doesn't sound so scary. If the word *forgive* sits in your craw, stop using it. Substitute *untie the knot,* and you'll find this week much easier.

"Forgiveness is the cash you need," says Hafiz in the poem that began today's Soul Play. It's the cash I need. It's the cash we all need to return to our true realm of divine freedom. Freedom—that's what we really want. That's the whole purpose of building a beautiful life, isn't it? Did you think it was the house, the car, the lover, the job, the contract, the money—all those things you want?

Think for a moment. What's the real reason you want the things you want? If you look beyond the things themselves, if you dig a little deeper, ask some bigger questions, you'll find that the underlying desire isn't the thing; it's the experience the thing can produce. For example, let's say you want money. If you were sitting right now on a five-foot high pile of money, would you be happy? Would that pile of money change your life? No, money is just printed paper. But start thinking of all the lovely things you could do with that money: send your child to college, give your parents a vacation, pay off your house, get out of debt, set up a business, provide a caregiver for someone in need. There is no end to the delightful things you could do with that pile of money.

So you see, it isn't the money you want—it's the freedom the money can create. That's what you want. To be free. To feel free. You want to "craft your falcon wings" and fly. You want to untie your knots and fly to the place where you are who you want to be, who you came here to be—the place where you are the fullest, richest expression of your whole, authentic, holy self.

Paradox Alert:
You don't want any thing;
you want the freedom the thing can produce.

Next week, you'll get clear about what you want to put on your wish list—your freedom list—but first you need some "cash" to spend. Imagine the universe for a moment as a divine department store. In this divine store, the golden currency is love, forgiveness, and gratitude.

Is there really anything else? Visualize people who love and are loved, who forgive and are forgiven, and whose hearts overflow with gratitude and joy. They are truly wealthy, aren't they? Their souls' bank accounts are brimming with divine tender. And they can "buy" anything they want. Well, you are going to place some large cosmic orders the day you create your Intention Mandala, so you need to gather some universe cash—quite a bit, in fact.

So decide right now, today, before you read another word: Do you want to untie your old knots? Do you want to be free? Are you ready to create space to be free? Are you willing to forgive to be free?

Reflect

- What do I think forgiveness is? Does "untie the knot" sound better to me?

- How do I feel about forgiveness being a currency of the universe?

- How would I rate my willingness to forgive on a scale from one to ten?

- Who or what are my biggest bugaboos about forgiveness?

- Do I think I can forgive this week? Am I willing to try?

- What do I think will happen? Am I expecting some benefit?

Write

Dear Voice,

A whole week of forgiveness—yuck! I get that unforgiveness is a living, breathing, black presence inside of me. I can see it and feel it. I can see that it keeps me tied to my old story. And I want to let that old story go so I can have a new story. But I confess that there are a few situations that I can't seem to forget and a few people I haven't been able to forgive. I know it's time to release them, but I'm not sure how. Help me get to that place where I can forgive, untie the knots, and be free. Because I really want to get my falcon wings and fly to my whole, authentic, holy self. How do we begin?

Explore

- Search inside yourself for clumps of anger, humiliation, resentment, jealousy, revenge, betrayal. Are those emotions taking up space inside you? Where do they reside? In your stomach, intestines, shoulders, neck, lungs, heart? When did they move in? How long have they been there?

- Sit with the idea of untying the knots of those negative emotions and watching them leave your body.

- Ask the idea of forgiveness to move from your brain to your heart. What happens when it enters your heart? Do you find you truly want to forgive and be free? When your heart says yes, you're ready—even if your mind isn't so sure.

- If your heart says no, have chats with your Voice about why you don't feel ready. If you don't feel ready, you don't feel ready. This is not a bad thing. It's where you are, and it's as real as a street corner. Be honest with yourself and the Voice. Ask big questions. They may feel like ouch questions, but if you enter into the conversation with an open heart and the desire to be free, you will be floored by the information that flows to you. Some questions that may help you locate a few tight knots are

- How much space is unforgiveness taking up inside of me?

- What benefits do I receive by not forgiving?

- What do I get out of keeping my resentment and anger alive?

- How has unforgiveness kept me tied up in my life? What has it prevented me from doing or experiencing?

- Why don't I feel ready to forgive?

- What needs to happen so that I can feel ready to forgive or at least move a bit closer to being ready?

- Lena Cestaro of Raleigh, North Carolina, asked, "How much space is my unforgiving taking up?" and received this answer, "A lot—so much that I am growing to fit it all." She had to laugh. Then she wrote, "What do I get out of keeping my resentment and anger alive?" The answer took her breath away: "I feel like I am punishing those people. But you are only hurting yourself. Those people are off living their lives, and you are sitting here, holding on to the negative feelings that are hurting you both emotionally and physically. It is like I want someone to pay for what was done to me even if that someone is me." Lena stared at the page. Those last six words were her breakthrough, and she was finally able to forgive.

- Have a conversation with your unforgiveness. See it inside you. See its color. Hear its name. Then speak to it on the page or out loud. Your unforgiveness may have something important to tell you. Don't fight it; tell it you welcome what it wants to say. Perhaps there are gifts hidden in your unforgiveness that you haven't found. Perhaps it has a message that you are finally ready to hear. Observe the conversation unfolding.

Don't judge it or edit it or try to control it. Your conversation might begin something like this:

Dear unforgiveness,
I see you. I feel where you live inside of me. I've been avoiding you for years, but now I want to have a conversation with you. I'm ready to hear what you have to say. I have been carrying you for a long, long time, so you must have something deeply important to teach me. Tell me. I am listening. With an open heart, I am listening.

- If ever there was a week for loving self-care, this is it. Be kind to your heart. Give it lots of quiet and solitude. Protect yourself from toxic people, thoughts, and media. Drink lots of water. Sleep all you can. You may be shocked at how weary you are. Releasing is physical and it can be exhausting.

Nourish

I untie the knot, and I am free.

Want More?

- Read the entire Hafiz poem "Forgiveness Is the Cash" in *The Subject Tonight Is Love* by Daniel Ladinsky.
- Read *Unconditional Forgiveness* by Mary Hayes Grieco or *Radical Forgiveness* by Colin Tipping.

call in the vultures

By far the strongest poison in the human spirit is the inability to forgive oneself or another person. It disables a person's emotional resources.

—Carolyn Myss, *Anatomy of the Spirit*

On the first day of my first forgiveness week, I was in my backyard writing. I had just started a conversation about forgiveness when a shadow passed over my journal. I looked up. A vulture was soaring directly over me, so close I could see her light brown underfeathers. I waved and said hello. Then her friends began to show up. Within seconds, there were thirteen majestic turkey vultures circling over my teeny tiny townhouse backyard.

There was no way it was an accident that the moment I began writing about forgiveness, thirteen vultures flew over me, but I wasn't sure what they were saying. So I went inside to get Ted Andrews' book *Animal Speak*. Like most people, I had a disgusting image of vultures: they eat dead things. Well, yes, they do, but, in the context of our week of forgiveness, eating dead things is exactly what we want. We want to untie the knots, release our unforgiveness, and have the vultures come and take the "dead" away for us. How beautiful is that?

According to *Animal Speak*, the vulture is a "truly wonderful creature" with much to teach us. In many cultures, it is a symbol of purification. The vulture has the power to dispel evil and help the person return to his or her true self. "Its medicine would restore harmony that had been broken," Andrews says. Well, that's what we want. We want to be restored to our whole self, the self that walks in harmony with Spirit and with the world. In the material world, the vulture purifies the area by eating all the decay and bacteria that could harm animals or people. A sweet clue about the turkey vulture's power is in its scientific name: *Cathartes aura* means "golden purifier."

Stay with this idea of purification for a moment. How does forgiveness purify us and our area?

The opposite—nonforgiveness—is toxic. We know this. We see it every day in people who cannot let go of their anger toward someone. And make no mistake, obsessive anger and resentment do make us sick. In *How God Changes Your Brain*, Andrew Newberg tells us that anger is "an insidious process that feeds on itself, and it can influence your behavior for very long periods of time. Eventually, it will even damage important structures in your brain. Nor is it good for your heart. . . . [A]nger, cynicism, hostility, and defensiveness will increase your risk of cardiovascular disease and cerebrovascular problems."

After reading about the vulture's power and symbolism, I went back to the page and asked for guidance on how to use vulture medicine to forgive. In light of what I learned, I developed the following ceremony to release unforgiveness to the vultures. If these steps feel right to you, use them. If not, design your own vulture-release ceremony.

Step 1: Stop Feeding Your Anger

Picture your thoughts as blood that feeds your anger like blood vessels feed a tumor. Stop feeding it. Stop talking about what happened. Stop obsessing about it. There is a famous Native American wisdom tale: A child was mean to a friend and ran to his grandfather to confess. The grandfather said there are two wolves fighting inside you. One is mean and greedy, and the other is peaceful and generous. The child asked which one would win. The elder said, "The one you feed."

If you're not ready to stop feeding your anger, it may be because you've never really told your story. Not fully—and not in the presence of the perfect listener. If that's the case, sit down with your divine partner and tell your story. Speak as you have never spoken before. Speak with heart, speak with power, speak with honor. Speak for the self you were and the self you are. Pour all the details onto the page. Hold back nothing. Release your deepest thoughts and feelings about this story.

In the loving, gentle presence of the Voice, keep digging. Don't settle for the story as you've told it for years. That story just keeps you prisoner. Dig underneath the details of your old story to find a deeper story. Explore the hidden emotions and desires. Ask big questions until the deeper meaning of the story bubbles to the surface.

When you've found that meaning—and it may take some time—say unequivocally:

> Thank you for listening. I am finished now. I understand my story in a new way. I see it in a new light. I have no need to tell that story again.

Step 2: Name the Gift in the Unforgiveable

Yes, there's a gift in there somewhere. If nothing else, it has brought you to the edge of forgiveness, and freedom lies on the other side. If Nelson Mandela can forgive after twenty-seven years of imprisonment, you can forgive. If the gift isn't clear, ask the vultures to help you find it:

> Vultures, help me find the gift in this pain. I still have hurt feelings, anger, frustration. I still feel a need for revenge. But I want to let go. So help me find the truth, the big "T" Truth, in this experience. Did I learn something? Did my spirit evolve through it? Was this a movement toward my wholeness? What possible good is there in this?

Step 3: Make a Conscious Decision
to Untie the Knot and Forgive

Say twice—first in writing on the page and then aloud in your own voice—that you want to forgive, are ready to forgive, and are calling on Spirit, your guides, your angels, and the vultures to come to your aid to help you do it:

> Dearest Spirit, I want to be free. I want to forgive _____.
> I am ready to forgive _____.

Step 4: Open Your Fist and Let Your Anger Go

You can visualize this experience of letting go in your mind, but it adds something to do it physically. The more sensual clues you send your soul, the more real the experience becomes. Write "I forgive _____ now and for all time" on a piece of paper. Hold the paper tight in your fist, feel the tension and anger of your history with that person move from your gut, through your arm and hand, and finally out onto the paper. Then open your hand and let the paper float to the ground. Burn it if you like. Or shred it. Or throw it in water. Or stick it under a rock. Do something to let that paper go.

Step 5: Call in the Vultures

Visualize your forgiveness vultures swooping in to consume the ashes or paper scraps or the invisible dust of hurt and anger floating in the air and, with it, all the bad bacteria of unforgiveness, vengeance, and pain.

Step 6: Thank the Vultures

Bless the vultures and thank them for purifying your body, your spirit, and your space. Now, turn around and walk forward to your true home, freedom.

How does the freedom of forgiveness feel? Do you feel lighter? Freer? Perhaps you have become so light, you can fly like a falcon to your true, whole, holy self. You certainly acquired some universe cash. You can't see it or feel it or count it, but it's there. Trust me, it's there.

Reflect

- How many years have I carried my old angry, hurt story?

- What do I get out of carrying it? Is there a gift in my old story?

- Could I have a new identity that doesn't involve this old story?

- Am I willing to stop telling this story? Am I ready to stop feeding this wound? Am I willing to start today?

- Am I ready to make a conscious decision to forgive?

Write

Dear Voice,

Oh boy, a "conscious decision to forgive." No beating round the bush. Yes or no. Forgive or stay angry. Sounds so simple. But let me tell you, it doesn't feel simple. I've been angry at _____ for a long time. How long? Let's see, it happened in _____. That's _____ years ago! I'm ready to stop feeding that story. No more blood flowing into this tumor. I get that. And I do love the idea of free, open space inside of me ready for something new. But you have to help me. Help me dig inside this story and find the gift so I can hand it to the vultures and say, "Here, you eat it. I want to be free." Help me.

Explore

- Be present for yourself today. Give yourself time and space to feel your feelings. If you need a good cry, have a good cry. If you feel anger welling up, feel it. It won't go away because you ignore it. Have compassion for yourself and your pain. In *You Are Here*, Thich Nhat Hanh reminds us, "There is no path to the cessation of suffering without suffering. The Buddha told us to embrace our suffering and to look at it deeply in order to understand its nature. Looking at suffering deeply, we will have deep insight into its nature, and the path of transformation and healing will present itself to us."

- To get to that path of transformation and healing, sit with your story. Honor your story. Tell your story to your divine partner one last time and really hear it. Feel it. You can also speak directly to your story:

  Dear sad story,
  I am here for you. Trying to chase you away hasn't worked. Ignoring you hasn't worked. And hoping you'll go away on your own hasn't worked. I see now that we have not really spoken. I am ready to listen. I am ready to embrace you. I have been carrying you inside me for so long, and the wound is still raw. You have something deeply important to tell me. Tell me. I am listening.

- If the weather permits, sit outside, especially if some vultures might fly over. Look up at the sky and imagine them there. Or, in your mind, invite them to visit you.

- If you prefer a different symbol for forgiveness, visualize that. It doesn't have to be vultures. They are simply the "blessengers" that came to me. Yours might be something else. Ask on the page or in an oracle-card reading or in your dreams for your own symbol to appear. Heaven will send your personal forgiveness blessengers.

- Heaven sent starlings to Victoria Strong in Paris, France. As Victoria sat in her window, getting ready for today's Soul Play, a cloud of starlings flew over her apartment. She named her blessengers "starbursts" and visualized them "bursting the toxins and carrying them to the stars to create space for forgiveness." Victoria had not seen starlings in such magnitude before or since.

- Once you know your blessenger, pay attention when it shows up. In the spring of 2010, I led a group of soul travelers to Costa Rica. One afternoon, a woman and I were sitting in an open gazebo on a huge expanse of green lawn under the Arenal volcano. Suddenly, a lone vulture swooped out of the sky and landed three feet from me. I knew why. I'd been saying some pretty judgmental things. I stood up, faced the vulture, and began talking to it. It walked around me as I spoke. I told the vulture I was wrong to judge. Finally, I said, "Thank you for your message. I am sorry. I won't do it again." It flew off. My companion stared at me, mouth agape. "Oh, that was just my friend the vulture," I said, "He came to remind me to judge not." The next morning at breakfast the woman whispered, "That vulture had a message about judgment for me, too."

- If you see vultures on the side of the road, bless them. Thank them for their important role in the cycle of life. Don't look away. Watch them do their cleansing work for a moment and visualize them cleaning up your own spiritual messes. Say thank you.

Nourish

I release what is dead, and the vultures take it away.

Want More?

Read about the vulture or any other blessenger in *Animal Speak* by Ted Andrews.

Day 17

the one you must forgive

Have you spoken with the little girl or little boy who is there, still alive in you? This little girl or little boy is suffering and carrying a lot of wounds. . . . Take the time to come back . . . and say, "Dear One, I am here for you. . . . I am here for myself. I am here for my suffering, for my pain." You should look at your pain as though it were an abandoned baby. You should come back to yourself so that you can take care of this suffering baby.

—Thich Nhat Hanh, *You Are Here*

Have you noticed that when you connect with your divine Voice on the page every day, those minutes expand until it seems every moment, no matter how mundane, becomes a vehicle for guidance, wisdom, and grace?

The day after the vultures arrived, I drove to my library to return a book. The street I took is a long row of ordinary cement-block houses. As I drove, I noticed a plain brown house out of the corner of my eye. I turned to look at it. I recognized that house. It had once belonged to my first post-divorce boyfriend. In the second it took to drive past his old house, I felt a twinge of neglect. He should have loved me more. And in that same instant, I felt an even stranger twinge. I should have been more lovable.

My head snapped back to the road, and my eyes popped open. I'd had no idea I was carrying any regret for that relationship, which I ended ten years ago. Why on earth was I feeling even the slightest speck of sorrow? And why on earth was I feeling that it was somehow my fault?

Paradox Alert:
Look for the extraordinary in the ordinary.

I realized, as I continued toward the library, that any time people pull away, even a little bit, even for all the right reasons, and even when we ask them to, we still feel at a subterranean level that, somehow, their departure was *our* fault. Somehow, we were not enough—not attractive enough, not smart enough, not successful enough, not rich enough, not sexy enough. It's a demented logic loop, I know. But here's how it sounds:

If I were good enough, people would love me.

They couldn't help it.

So, if someone does not love me totally, madly, and completely,

I must not be good enough.

It sounds pretty comical laid out like that. But don't laugh. Look instead for the wounded truth inside the loop. Go ahead—test it for yourself. Pick a relationship that didn't work out. If you peek behind the door, I think you'll find that at a deep, irrational emotional level, you feel that somehow you didn't hold the person's attention. If you had been just a wee bit more something, then he or she would not have turned to someone else, or fallen out of love with you, or simply stopped being interested.

Why is this such a big message? And why is it so important for this week? Because it proves that there is really only one person who needs forgiving: you. Not the other guy—you. It's always you. The wound is inside of you. It's not about what the other guy did—that can and will be forgiven. But the first wound, the greatest wound, and the hardest one to heal, is inside of you.

Have you noticed that?

Reflect

- When I think about relationships that have ended, do I feel like the other person should have loved me more?
- Do I feel the fact that they didn't love me enough is somehow my fault, because I wasn't lovable enough?
- Am I the person I most need to forgive?
- Do I feel I need to forgive myself? What have I done that I haven't or can't forgive myself for?
- Do I want to forgive myself?
- Do I know how to forgive myself?

Write

Dear Voice,

I am the one I need to forgive. I get this idea for sure. But in some ways forgiving myself is tougher than forgiving the other guy, and lord knows that one is hard. Let's talk about this. Do I think I somehow didn't hold people close enough? What about ____? And ____? Do I feel deep inside that I wasn't lovable enough? Is that what I want to forgive myself for? Help me understand why I'm the one who must be forgiven—and how to do that.

Explore

- Be fully present for yourself today. Don't let the world pull you into its endless escape hatches of television, food, drink—whatever. Don't go back to sleep!

- If exploring the idea of forgiving yourself feels too hard to do on your own, call on your wise self, your GrandSelf, the one who knows that everything, including this struggle to forgive yourself, is a movement toward your wholeness. Ask your GrandSelf to communicate with the self struggling to forgive.

- Write your little boy or little girl a love letter. Tell the wounded child inside of you that you are here and you understand. And soon all shall be well. The sweet wash of forgiveness is at hand.

Nourish

I forgive myself.

Want More?

Read *You Are Here* by Thich Nhat Hanh.

Day 18

enough

The discerning voice can also show a darker side and turn in on itself to become a voice of self-criticism and make your heart into a place of torment. Harsh and unrelenting, it finds fault with everything. . . . This voice can assume complete control in determining how you see yourself and the world. It can make you blind to the beauty in you.

—John O'Donohue, *Beauty*

Was yesterday's realization that the person who needs to be forgiven is you a bit surprising? Did it make you cry? That's normal. When people feel that realization strike deep in their heart, tears invariably well up. These are good tears. These tears are little messages bobbing up from your soul saying, "Yes, oh yes! Please forgive yourself. There is so much ahead of us, so much beauty, so much potential, so much joy. But as long as you have these heavy scars in your heart, you can't see all that good. And because you can't see it, you can't have it. So, yes, please forgive yourself. Because the truth is you are so much more beautiful than you know."

I've struggled long and hard with this idea of not being enough. And I know you have, too. Why do we struggle? Why does it take years—and for many, a lifetime—to come to the awareness that we are enough?

It's because of our brains. "Unfortunately as far as the brain is concerned, negative speech has a stronger effect than positive speech," writes Andrew Newberg in *How God Changes*

Your Brain. "Negative remarks and memories are more strongly encoded in the brain, and they are the most difficult memories to eradicate." When the adults in your childhood said stinging words that left you feeling dumb or foolish or unloved, your brain hardwired those messages into itself. Now the only person who can alter that wiring is you.

I wrote a prayer-poem called "Enough" years ago, and the words still resonate. They sound like slow, deep vibrations from a bell that has been ringing for a long, long time. I am ready to stop clanging the bell of not enough. I'm going to say this prayer one more time. Today. Out loud. With vigor. I'm going to feel it in my bones and know that it is true. From this day forward, I am enough. I am more than enough.

This prayer is for you, too.

Enough

Dear God of the universe, creator of all life, hear me.
This one prays.

In the mirror—in the reflection that bounces from me to the world and back again,
there is a circle, a circle of sadness.

I am not enough.
They see not enough; therefore, I am not enough—

    not good enough
    not strong enough, perhaps,
    not smart enough, for sure,
    not handsome enough,
    not pretty enough,
    not wealthy enough, never wealthy enough,
    not fast enough,
    not clever enough
    not tough enough, but too tough sometimes, and that makes me
    not kind enough,
    something not enough,
    many things not enough.

Perhaps it doesn't matter what. The specific fault is irrelevant.
It's enough just to know that I'm not enough of whatever it is I'm not enough of.

Do you understand this, God? Seems a bit convoluted, I know.
But circles are circles, and everywhere I turn there are more of them.

If I look at my work, I'm not good enough,
    and, of course, they see I'm not good enough.
    Therefore, I'm not good enough.
    And doesn't my "success" just prove it?

If I look at my family, I'm not loving enough.
    They know I could love them more.
    Just look at our tensions, and you'll see that I'm right.
    I'm not loving enough.

If I look in the mirror, I'm not pretty enough.
    There it is for the world to see: blemishes, imperfections, crooked teeth,
    blotchy skin, ridiculous hair, flaccid muscles. I think I'll stop now.
    But you see. Well, I see. I'm not pretty enough.

If I look in my checkbook, I'm not rich enough.
    Doesn't take a banker to see I don't earn enough.
    Perhaps if I worked harder, smarter, faster, better, *something*, I'd be better off.
    But there it is. I'm not rich enough.

I could continue, but I need to move on.
There are things to do, people to see, problems to solve.
And I'm not organized enough to get it all done.

So I have to get going.
But first, I need to ask you this question. It's important.
Why did you put me here, if I'm not enough?

Why didn't you make me pretty enough, smart enough, rich enough?
You could have, you know.
Even now, you could do it in a single breath:

    Ask, and poof, I am beautiful
    Ask, and poof, I am wealthy
    Ask, and poof, I am smart

Ask, and I'm wanted
Ask, and I'm wise
Ask, and I'm . . .

What?
What do I want?
What do I *really* want?

Want beyond wanting?
Need beyond needing?
What is the hole that must be filled?

Love, I guess.
Yes, Love.
That's it, isn't it?

If I had Love, enough Love, I would be blessed.
If I had Love, the right Love, I would be joyous.
If I had perfect Love, pure Love—your Love—I would be healed.

That's what I ask for, dear God.
That's what I want. Love is what I need.
Starting here. With me. Just me.

Fill me with the Love of the angels.
Build a bridge of Love across my doubts and fears.
Pour Love all around me in my eyes, my mouth, my heart, and my mind.

It feels good, this Love, warm and calm and easy.
It has no ambition, but it won't stay still.
It needs nothing, yet it sets my heart in motion.

This Love is peaceful, yet yearns to spread.
It oozes out of me and fills the room.
It swims out of the room and fills the house.
It radiates out of the house and seeks the world.

I guess it is enough, isn't it!
Enough for me. Enough for now.
Enough for always and ever.

Enough.

Amen.

Do you feel that sweet love flowing in you and through you? Be still and let it settle into every cell of your body. Step inside your heart and look around. What do you see?

When I wrote this poem, I saw and felt and even smelled glorious pink light. It smelled like roses. It took me awhile to recognize what this feeling is. It's unconditional love—that love we all want and struggle so to find. It's here. You have it. Recognize it. Hold onto it. It's in you, and that means you can send it to anyone you want. When you want to pray for someone, visualize a pink stream of unconditional love leaving you and flowing to that person. And don't forget to give it to yourself. Send it in a little pink circle out and around and back to you. Send it when you're feeling sad or frightened. Send it when you're feeling happy. Send it all the time. Because you are not only enough, you are the beloved of the Divine.

Reflect

- Does "Enough" speak to me? What parts? What lines?
- If I look at myself in the mirror, or at my work, my checkbook, or my family, do I feel I'm not enough? How am I not enough?
- Where did that idea come from? When did it start? Is this a thought worm?
- How about the second part of the prayer-poem? Is love what I really want? Is it?
- Do I want to ask for divine love?
- If I felt full of divine love, would I feel like I am enough?

Write

Dear Voice,

Oh, this hurts. I've lived with this not-enough thing for so very long. I got the idea as a kid. I clearly heard that I

wasn't ___ enough. I never felt like people thought I was ___
enough. I resonate with Janet's poem. Made me cry, to tell the
truth. So let's talk about this. Feeling like I'm not enough is
a big gaping hole, and I want to fill it. I want to walk around
knowing I am enough. Talk to me. How am I enough?

Explore

- Read "Enough" out loud. Or listen to me read it at
  my website.

- Feel the feeling of not being enough. But then move
  into the different place, the enough place. Call on the
  Divine to fill you with big love. Visualize a living river
  of the pink light of love headed to you and through
  you, lifting you and loving you.

- If you need help, call on your guides and angels to
  love you, to be with you, to let you know that you are
  not only enough, but you are also more than enough—
  you are beautiful. Call in the vultures to remove any
  not-enough feelings.

- Go to the mirror, look yourself in the eye, and
  say something like this: "Hey beautiful, you are so
  enough!" If you flinch (and most people do), say it
  again. And again. Say it until you can grin back and
  shout, "I am so enough!"

- Be aware of your dreams. They might be profound.

- Pay attention to the emotional charge of your words.
  According to Andrew Newberg in *How God Changes Your
  Brain*, "[E]motionally positive words like love, compassion, and trust activate the . . . parts of the brain that
  are related to pleasure, happiness, peace and the sense
  of impending reward." Resolve to use more positive language when you speak to yourself and to those
  around you.

Nourish

I am enough.

Want More?

Read chapter 7, "What Happens When God Gets Mad? Anger, Fear, and the Fundamentalist in Our Brain," in *How God Changes Your Brain* by Andrew Newberg, MD.

Day 19

release your prisoners

If it should happen therefore that while you are presenting your offering upon the altar, and right there you remember that your brother has any grievance against you, leave your offering there upon the altar, and first go and make peace with your brother, and then come back and present your offering.

—Jesus, Matthew 5:23–24
(Holy Bible from the Ancient Eastern Text)

We've been talking about forgiveness for several days now, and the conversation keeps getting richer. Truth is, we could talk about forgiveness for months and still find more to learn and more to forgive. That's why most people don't start. We sense instinctively that if we begin to poke beneath the "I'm fine" mask we show the world, we'll find dozens of wounds that need healing, and there would be no end to the forgiveness work. So why start?

Here's why: forgiveness is the most delicious, most healing, most soul-lifting, joy-inducing thing you can do.

Want freedom? *Forgive.*

Want a vibrant healthy body? *Forgive.*

Want to find your purpose? *Forgive.*

Want to feel joy? *Forgive.*

Want to love and be loved? *Forgive.*

Want a magical, vibrant, abundant life? *Forgive!*

Forgiveness is the magic or, as Hafiz says, "the cash." It opens the door to a life you cannot even imagine at the moment—a life that's yours, all yours, if you will just let go of the anger and resentment holding you prisoner. St. Teresa of Avila knew the magic of forgiveness in the sixteenth century. She explained it in her spiritual masterpiece *The Interior Castle*, in which she describes the soul as a castle with seven floors. Author Caroline Myss, in her own 2008 book, *Entering the Castle*, shares her modern insights into St. Teresa's teachings. She writes that in the basement of everyone's soul castle, there is a dank, cold dungeon where we hold our prisoners.

> As you walk through, notice that there are cells for prisoners lining the walls. Everyone you cannot forgive or whom you resent or wish harm to is held by you in these cells. The parents you cannot forgive are in a cell; the business partner who cheated you and whom you still resent is in a cell; the ex-spouse is in a cell. . . . No doubt some of the people you hold prisoners are holding you prisoner as well. . . .Why do you keep prisoners? [Y]ou keep someone or something prisoner because you feel he has not yet been punished enough for the harm he did to you.

It's time to take a tour of your dungeon. Read the following "Release Your Prisoners" process to understand it; then close your eyes and visualize going through it. I also offer it as a guided meditation you can find as an audio file on my website. If you feel wobbly on your feet, do it sitting or lying down.

Release Your Prisoners

Stand up to stretch out your dungeon—your lower gut. Put your hands in front of your dungeon, as if they were two heavy doors. Close your eyes.

Then slowly open your hands. As they open, see the long, cold, dim stairway leading down to your dungeon. Slowly walk down the stone steps. The air gets colder and colder as you descend. There is barely enough light to see. Be careful. Don't slip. Touch the wall to help you.

At the bottom of the stairs is a huge, old, heavily scarred wooden door, the entrance to your dungeon. Haul it open. You are the only one who can.

As the door creaks open, stale putrid air assaults you. The smell is unbearable. The air is even colder and damper than that of the stairway. There is very little light. As your eyes adjust, step over the threshold.

You are now in your dungeon. Look around. Notice the black prison cells lining the walls of your dungeon. You may be surprised at how many there are.

Walk up to the first cell. Look at your prisoner. You see who it is. You know why you locked up this prisoner and when. This prisoner has been in your dungeon a long time. Now it's time to let your prisoner go.

Reach out and open the cell door. You are the only one who can. Look your prisoner in the eye for a moment; then motion for your prisoner to leave. Wave your arm; point to the door. No talking. You don't have to explain. You don't have to go over the old story. You don't even have to apologize. Just let your prisoner go. Your prisoner may hesitate. Wave your prisoner away, saying silently, "You are free. You can go now. Go. Go."

Walk up to the next cell. Look at your prisoner. You know who it is. Open the door. Motion for your prisoner to leave. "You're free. Go now. Go."

Then walk up to the next cell. You know what to do: recognize your prisoner, open the door, and let your prisoner go. Do that.

Then go to the next cell and the next and the next. Let all your prisoners go.

When all your prisoners have gone, stop and look around at the rows of empty cells.

But wait. You're not finished. You have one more prisoner.

Walk to the very back of your dungeon. Look. There in the corner, in the darkest, dankest, coldest, most miserable cell, is your longest suffering prisoner. Look at your prisoner. Look. Do you see who it is?

It's you. It's always been you. You have kept yourself prisoner for years. You've held yourself prisoner for all the things you think you cannot be forgiven for.

Open the cell. Open it! Say to your prisoner-self, "Up. Up. Get up now. You're free." And let yourself go.

Now, at last, your dungeon is empty. Look at all the vacant cells. Lean back slightly and call on the loving power of Spirit to flood your dungeon with white and gold light. Watch as the cells dissolve and the space is filled with warm, loving, healing light. When the space is completely transformed from dark to light, from cold to warm, from prison to chapel, say thank you and open your eyes.

Sit down and rest after this experience. Take a moment to register how you feel. Then deep soul write about it. There are few experiences more profound than releasing your prisoners.

I include this "Release Your Prisoners" experience in several of my courses and live events. It amazing that something so short and simple can be so effective. It is a miracle unto itself that without retelling, rehashing, or revisiting your painful stories, and without even apologizing, you can experience real release in a matter of minutes.

Paradox Alert:
When you hold others prisoner,
you hold yourself prisoner.

That release is available every time you return to empty your dungeon. Deborah Gardiner of Houston sent this touching report after experiencing the "Release Your Prisoners" meditation for the fourth time.

The first time, I released my ex and all that baggage. These last three rounds have been about releasing myself through an age progression. I held myself hostage first as a young child, then again at age twelve. Tonight, I was brought to tears when I found myself being held prisoner down there at age thirty-four. It seems I have a lifelong pattern of blaming and beating myself up. Is it any wonder my thought worm was "I am not worthy"? Thank you so much for helping me let myself go.

I know "Release Your Prisoners" works, but until Linda Bryant, a freelance writer in Nashville, came to a Lotus and the Lily course, I had no idea just how miraculous it could be. When the class opened, Linda had lost her major clients and didn't have any new work. On top of her financial woes, her foot was badly broken, her health was deteriorating, and she was deeply depressed and swamped with medical bills. In desperation, she'd begun to sell her grandmother's jewelry to buy groceries. When I led the group in this meditation, Linda was shocked to see that her dungeon was crammed with prisoners. She released a few that night, but there were dozens more. The next day, she began an ongoing process to identify all her prisoners. There were seventy-five! Some, like her first grade teacher, had committed minor offenses, but others were guilty of years of abuse and neglect. Her worst prisoner was her father.

Linda realized she needed to not only get her prisoners out, but also get them to *stay* out. So she created a City of Forgiveness for them. When Linda identified a prisoner, she opened that cell and asked that prisoner to leave. If that prisoner didn't want to leave, she escorted him to the City of Forgiveness.

Some of her prisoners fought hard to stay in the prison. Her deceased mother was one who would not leave. In deep soul writing, Linda asked her mother why she wouldn't leave. Her mother answered, "I want you to understand that you're doing to yourself what I was doing to you." Once Linda acknowledged that message, her mother walked out of her prison cell and stepped into the City of Forgiveness. Slowly, the prison emptied. Over time, so did the city. As our course drew to a close, Linda felt moved to put a photograph of her father on her altar. She sensed that until she could forgive him, she would never be free.

When we got together thirty days after the course ended, Linda had several miracles to report. Since clearing out her dungeon, she had so many new writing assignments she was giving the excess to other writers. And she was given a beautiful writing space in an historic building in downtown Nashville—for free. And her foot was healing beautifully. And her big dream had come true: she'd been accepted into a prestigious MFA program.

As astonishing as all those miracles were, they paled in comparison to the last. Her father called one day and said he'd like to help pay for the MFA. "You must understand," Linda told us, "my father is the original Scrooge; he's never given anyone anything."

When I checked in with Linda a year later, she said that forgiveness is still the center of her life, and it's still a font of miracles. She said, "My feelings still get hurt, but now, as quickly as the hurt feelings come up, the thought 'Oh, here's somebody to forgive' comes. I admit the hurt, angry feelings I'm having, but then I'm willing to go into forgiveness." Then she gave me a clue to the even deeper gifts of forgiveness:

I never could relate when people said they felt humble or had humility. Over the past year, I have this feeling of being humbled by the difference between how dysfunctional and imperfect interactions with people can be and how much love and forgiveness is actually available inside me despite these other feelings. To just touch the possibility of that is humbling.

A few days after our conversation, Linda sent an email with the biggest and most important forgiveness news of all: "I just spent Thanksgiving with my father. He hasn't changed one iota, and yet I felt more loving than ever. Forgiveness clears out the space for love!"

Reflect

- Who is in my dungeon? Any surprise prisoners?
- Do I want to empty my dungeon? Really?
- Do I think it's that easy, just let my prisoners go?
- Can I let all my prisoners go? Or are there some I want to keep locked up?
- What do I think will happen when I let my prisoners go?
- Am I in other people's dungeons? In lots of people's?
- How does it feel to know that I am locked in someone's dungeon?

Write

Dear Voice,

I like the simplicity of this exercise. I'm just going to open the cells and let my prisoners out—with your help, of course. Let's do this. Let's do this together. I'll take you on a tour of my dungeon and together we'll open all the cells. I'm ready. I'm so ready. I don't want to drag this clanking dungeon around any more. I want to release my prisoners and be released from their dungeons, too. Okay, let's go. We're walking down the stairs. I'm opening the door. I'm showing you my dungeon . . .

Explore

- Empty your dungeon in your mind or on the page in dialogue with your Voice—or both.

- If you have prisoners who won't leave, ask them to tell you what they want to say. Like Linda's mom, your prisoner may have a critical message for you.

- You can release your prisoners in other ways. For example, you can ask Archangel Michael to cut the psychic cords binding you and someone together. Ask your guides and angels to help you come up with a special release experience.

- Whatever release method you use, the important thing is to do it, not just think about it. Do it until it feels complete. Don't be concerned if it takes repetition. When asked how many times to forgive, Jesus said, "Seven times seventy" (Matthew 18:22).

- Don't forget to say thank you. Thank your divine partners and guides for their loving support and guidance.

- Rest. Releasing your prisoners is more exhausting than you realize. When you release your prisoners from the cells of your dungeon, you are releasing poison from the cells of your body.

Nourish

I release my prisoners.

Want More?

In addition to *Entering the Castle,* Caroline Myss has also written *Anatomy of the Spirit* and *Sacred Contracts,* in which she connects the energetic dots between unforgiveness and disease and between forgiveness and health. Her audiobook *Spiritual Madness* is also superb. If you are experiencing a dark night of the soul, listen to it. During my divorce, I listened to it so often the tapes wore out—twice!

Day 20

finally forgive

Hatred does not cease by hatred, but only by love;
this is the eternal rule.

—The Buddha

Is clearing our hearts, brains, and bodies of the silent—or not so silent—anger and resentment really necessary? Ask yourself. You know if you have old, crusty crud blocking your spiritual arteries. You know if you're carrying a pocketful of anger toward some jerk who done you wrong. You know if deep inside you still wish that something rotten would happen to someone. You know. And you know if this anger is getting in the way. You know how it has gotten in the way in the past, and you know how it is getting in the way of calling in a beautiful life.

So once and for all, it's time to untie the knot. Let go. Move on. Release. Forgive. It's time to finally, totally, and completely forgive.

Want to do that? Well, it's your lucky day because it just so happens I know how.

No, let me amend that. It isn't that I *know* how to forgive. I'm not sure anyone, no matter how many books he's read or written, really knows how. But those of us who have had a profound experience of forgiveness do know something special: we know that forgiveness is miraculous. We know that when we forgive—not in the mind or even in the heart, but at the deepest, subatomic soul-body level—something happens. Chains really do break. Spirits really are released. Two people are instantly and miraculously free.

So can I explain how "Finally Forgive," the forgiveness prayer I am about to give you, breaks those chains? No, not really. It's a mystical experience. It's a miracle. All I can tell you is that it does.

I wrote "Finally Forgive" on March 25, 2001, but I spent several years of kicking and screaming and resisting forgiveness before I was ready to do so. If you've read *Writing Down Your Soul,* you know that my divorce between 1996 and 1999 was frightening. For longer than I care to admit, I prayed that God would do some serious smiting of my ex-husband, his smarmy lawyer, and the evil judge they had in their hooks.

During the peak of my fear in 1998, a friend gave me a tape set of a live Carolyn Myss *Anatomy of the Spirit* weekend workshop in Orlando. One night, I settled into my living room chair in the dark to begin listening to it. As Myss concluded the opening session, she introduced Ron Roth, a healer and former priest, to give a blessing. In the dark in my living room, I followed the directions he gave: put out your hands and visualize a little image of yourself on your left hand and an image of the person with whom you have the greatest difficulty on your right hand. I immediately pictured a tiny version of my husband in my right hand. Now, Roth said, hold both hands up to God and know that God loves the person in your right hand as much as God loves you.

I snatched my hands back and burst into tears. God loved my ex-husband! Oh, how this realization hurt! But I knew it was true. From then on, I stopped begging God to punish my ex and started begging God to show me how to live. That night, I took the first baby step toward forgiveness.

Four years later, I was sitting in the front row of a Sunday service at Unity Church of Clearwater in Florida. The minister, Rev. Leddy Hammock, opened her lesson with a reading I'd never heard before: "It is someone who is forgiven little who shows little love" (Luke 7:47). My heart burst open. In that moment, I knew I had to forgive my ex-husband—finally and completely, forgive him. So he could love again. So I could love again. So he could love our son more. So I could love our son more. At long last, I wanted—actually wanted—my ex-husband to be free to love and be loved. I was finally, really, truly, and completely ready to forgive.

Sitting there in church, I pulled out my journal and a pen and started to write, and "Finally Forgive" came out on the page, fully formed.

Here it is. I offer this prayer to you as a gift. Perhaps "Finally Forgive" will help you to also finally forgive. For now, just read it. If it speaks to your heart, the "Explore" section has suggestions on how you can personalize it and turn it into a blessing for yourself and someone you wish to forgive. If you'd like to hear me read this prayer, visit my website.

Finally Forgive

A prayer of finally, really, truly, and completely choosing to forgive

Part I: The Gap

There is a gap between you and me.
In the gap is pain and fear and anger.
In the gap is our history of ugly thoughts, ugly words, ugly actions.
In the gap are the sounds of screaming, crying and swearing.
That gap is killing us and hurting our child.

What good is there in that gap?
What good is there in refusing to cross it?
What good is there in staying angry?
What good is there in not forgiving?

Part II: One Love

If there really is only one love—God's love—then:
How can I love my work,
    if I don't love you, in some way? Just a little.

How can I love our son with my whole heart,
if I don't love you, in some way? Just a little.

How can I love my new relationship,
whomever that may be, whenever that may be,
if I don't love you, won't love you, can't love you, in some way? Just a little.
How can I love my home, my family, my friends?
How can I love my purpose, my reason for being,
if I don't love you, in some way?

If I could love you, just a little,
I could love my life all the more,
love my child all the more,
love my work, my home, my friends, all the more.

Part III: The Choice

I have it in my power to hate you, to ignore you, to blame you.
I have it in my power to make your life difficult, set up little traps, say small nasty things.
I have it in my power to paint you as the bad guy, the stupid one, the fool.
And, I have it in my power to forgive you, to love you, in some way. Just a little.

The truth is your presence in my life was a gift.
For now and for always, you gave me our precious child,
the sweetest gift on earth.
And you taught me, finally taught me, to say no.

Thanks to you, I learned, oh God, how I learned.
Thanks to you, I grew, till I became bigger, stronger, richer, fuller.
Thanks to you, I walked. I walked a long tough journey, but I walked
to this place, this moment, when I know who I am.
I know what I'm thinking. I know what I'm feeling.
And I see a clear choice:

I can hold you in this corner, where you are forever wrong.
Or, I can hold you in the light, where you are free to grow, and change, and be happy.

Dear God, I'm choosing.
I'm closing the gap, filling it with forgiveness,

day 20

plugging the holes, and posting a sign:

Only love is spoken here.

Reflect

- Am I ready to choose to forgive? Totally? Completely?
- Am I doing it because I expect something to happen?
- Am I willing and ready to forgive even if nothing—or at least nothing apparent—happens?
- What would my life look like if "only love were spoken here"?
- How would "only love is spoken here" change my thoughts, words, actions?

Write

Dear Voice,

I am ready. I can do this. I think so, anyway. But before I do, I'd like to talk it over with you one last time. I had no idea going into this week just how powerful it would be. I went deeper than I ever imagined. I thought I understood the importance of forgiveness, but I see now that I had no idea just how profound and important forgiveness is. But at long last, I am ready to step forward and make the final choice. I am ready to choose to release someone I've been angry with for a long, long time. I am ready to hold _____ up to the light. I want _____ to be free to grow in the light. I do. Because I want to be free to grow in the light, too. I want both of us to be free, so we can both grow and be happy. I'm ready. Please be with me as I finally forgive.

Explore

- If "Finally Forgive" speaks to you, take it, say it, pray it. Personalize it, change the words. Massage the prayer until it feels good. Or write your own prayer of forgiveness. On the page, ask the Voice how to write it. You will receive your own unique passage into the freedom of forgiveness.

- When you are ready, speak your prayer out loud. There is something that happens when we pray out loud. "When you speak with 100 percent of your being, your speech becomes mantra. In Buddhism, a mantra is a sacred formula that has the power to transform reality," says Thich Nat Hanh in *You Are Here*. Well, there's nothing as transformative as forgiveness, so put your whole self into this prayer. Say it with conviction, with meaning, with heart. Hold up your hands as you look at the left and right corners of the room and make your choice with conviction. It is the most important choice you can make.

- Don't be surprised if you feel light headed when you say your prayer out loud. If you sense something happened, something did. Be still. Rest in the sweet feeling of freedom. Say thank you. This is a precious time to deep soul write.

- If you don't feel ready to forgive, don't force yourself. You are where you are. When you're ready, you'll find your own way to finally, totally, and completely forgive.

Nourish

I choose to forgive.

Want More?

The Ho'oponopono from the Huna in Hawaii is a lovely and powerful forgiveness practice composed of four seemingly simple sentences: "I'm sorry. Please forgive me. Thank you. I love you."

Day 21

finally
forgive yourself

Awake, my dear.
Be kind to your sleeping heart.
Take it out into the vast fields of Light
And let it breathe.

Say,
"Love,
Give me back my wings.
Lift me,
Lift me nearer."

—Hafiz, from "Awake Awhile," *I Heard God Laughing,*
Translation by Daniel Ladinsky

Before we close our week, there's one more act of forgiveness. This one will finally free you and get those falcon wings sprouting.

After the rich experience of forgiving another, did you wonder what it would feel like to offer the same absolution to yourself? You might have done it ages ago if it weren't for the heavy chains holding you down: guilt, shame, blame. There's a problem with these negative emotions. "[I]f you blame yourself, guilt can shut your frontal lobes down. If that happens, you lose your ability to analyze the situation, and the longer you stay focused on negative self-beliefs, the more likely you are to become depressed," says Andrew Newberg in *How God Changes Your Brain*.

A woman on the first Writing Down Your Soul soul venture in Oaxaca, Mexico, came face to face with these chains. After a group discussion about forgiveness, she went back to her room and had an intense conversation on the page. She went over all the mistakes she'd made and told her Voice she couldn't forgive herself for the botch she'd made of her life. The Voice stopped her and wrote, "How can you condemn what I have already forgiven?"

Sit with that sentence. Take it into your heart. It's a message for you, too.

Here's a way to forgive yourself. Say this version of "Finally Forgive" to and for yourself. As you read it, look into your eyes in the mirror. You can also hear me read it at my website.

Finally Forgive

A prayer of finally, really, truly, and completely choosing to forgive myself

Part I: The Gap

There is a gap inside me.
In the gap is pain and fear and anger.
In the gap is my history of ugly thoughts, ugly words, ugly actions.
In the gap are the sounds of screaming, crying and swearing.
That gap is killing me and hurting my life.

What good is there in that gap?
What good is there in refusing to cross it?
What good is there in staying angry?
What good is there in not forgiving myself?

Part II: One Love

If there really is only one love—God's love—then:
How can I love my work,
     if I don't love myself?

How can I love my child with my whole heart,
    if I don't love myself?

How can I love a new relationship, whomever that may be, whenever that may be,
    if I don't love myself, won't love myself, can't love myself?
How can I love my home, my family, my friends?
How can I love my purpose, my reason for being,
    if I don't really and fully love myself?

If I could love myself that way,
I could love my life all the more,
love my child all the more
love my work, my home, my friends, all the more.

Part III: The Choice

I have it in my power to hate myself, to ignore myself, to blame myself.
I have it in my power to make my own life difficult, set up little traps,
say small nasty things.
I have it in my power to paint myself as the bad guy, the stupid one, the fool.
And, I have it in my power to forgive myself, to love myself, to embrace myself.

The truth is my life is a gift.
For now and for always, life gave me _____ (put in life's richest gifts),
the sweetest gifts on earth.
And my life taught me, finally taught me, to say no.

Thanks to life, I learned, oh God, how I learned.
Thanks to life, I grew, till I became bigger, stronger, richer, fuller.
Thanks to life, I walked. I walked a long tough journey, but I walked
to this place, this moment, when I know who I am.
I know what I'm thinking. I know what I'm feeling.
And I see a clear choice:

I can hold myself in this corner, where I am forever wrong.
Or I can hold myself in the light, where I am free to grow, and change, and be happy.

Dear God, I'm choosing.
I'm closing the gap, filling it with forgiveness,
plugging the holes, and posting a sign:
Only love is spoken here.

Reflect

- How long have I been angry at myself for my mistakes?
- Am I ready to finally forgive myself?
- What's holding me back? Do I think I don't deserve to be forgiven? Am I waiting for someone else to forgive me?
- How important is it that I forgive myself?
- What would it look like if I only spoke with love to myself?

Write

Dear Voice,

If I thought yesterday was rich, just look at today! I am ready. I can do this. I must do this. If there's one thing I learned this week, it's that I'm one of the most important people who must be forgiven. I thought I had forgiven myself, but reading this version of "Finally Forgive," I realize there's still self-judgment in there, disgust at my choices. Like that woman in Oaxaca, "How could I have been so stupid?" keeps coming to the surface to try to prevent me from freeing myself. But I am determined. I want love to lift me higher. I will not be my own prisoner. I will totally and completely forgive myself. Help me. Lift me. Lift me higher.

Explore

- If this self-forgiveness version of "Finally Forgive" speaks to you, say it. Or change it or write your own self-forgiveness prayer.
- Be very kind to your heart today. This self-forgiveness prayer is the richest prayer of all. Gently untie the knot of self-judgment. Release those chains. And be free.

Nourish

I totally and completely forgive myself.

Want More?

No one writes more elegantly and gently about self-forgiveness than Thich Nhat Hanh. If you have any of his books, spend time with him today.

The Second Wave: Gratitude

Our week of creating space for the new by untying and releasing the old has come to an end. What happened for you this week? Did these experiences move you a bit closer to wholeness? When you look inside yourself, do you see new space? How do you feel? Different? Lighter? Are your falcon wings sprouting? And what about all that universe cash you got for trading in your unforgiveness? Are you aware of it growing in your celestial bank accounts?

You have much to be grateful for. Even if you don't feel complete, be grateful for what happened this week. You probably feel there's still more to do. There is. There are always more people to forgive, more situations to bless, more judgments to release, and more piles of dead stuff to give to the vultures. Forgiveness is not a one-time event; it's a spiritual practice—a life-long spiritual practice. It's a way of living. So even if you sense you haven't released everything, I invite you to stop and celebrate what you have released. Say thank you for a new awareness of the miracle of forgiveness. Be grateful for the prayers and tools you found. Be grateful for the vultures and guides who helped you. Be grateful for every knot you untied. So what if there are twenty more? You can, and you will, untie them—maybe next week, maybe next year. For today, be grateful for where you are. Remember, only love is spoken here—especially to yourself.

Stand with your Soul Slinky and recall that wave of intention you sent out a few days ago. Contemplate the rich week that has transpired and send a reciprocal wave of gratitude. Tomorrow you can begin looking forward to the beautiful life ahead. But for today, honor and celebrate where you are. Give yourself a gift—a lovely meal, a walk in the park—something delightful.

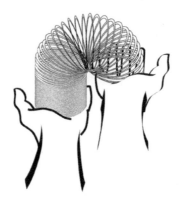

look forward

You've accumulated a rich array of experience and wisdom in the last three weeks. Your interior life is blooming, and your cosmic accounts are overflowing. You may not have realized it, but you received a nice deposit when you began this adventure to create a beautiful life. And while you were busy looking back, the universe was busy filling your accounts. Last week you collected mounds of universe cash in the form of forgiveness. This week you start thinking about what you want to spend it on.

But please don't visualize yourself at a store counter, looking at something wonderful, say a new job, handing over some cash, and walking away with a shiny new job. In the Lotus and the Lily, we are moving beyond that simple application of attraction into a multidimensional process that creates a *whole* beautiful life. You will still get that new job using this process, but it may be something far more delightful than you currently imagine.

We've all had that "store counter" experience of asking for something and suddenly receiving it. It's fun. And it's a lovely reminder that the universe really is a miraculous place and it really does respond to us. But have you noticed that things don't always work out? Let's say you want something. You want it a lot. You ask for it. You get it. But once you have it, you look at the thing, the person, the job—whatever it was you so desperately wanted—and you desperately wish you could return it.

A few years ago, I'd gone to Wisconsin to help my mother move out of her house and into an assisted-living facility. As I waited in the Central Wisconsin Airport for the first leg of my flight back to Tampa, I started writing in my journal. I told Spirit I felt ready to date. I began writing about what I wanted. Race? Someone comfortable in his skin. Profession? Someone who loved his work. Children? A man who deeply loved his children. Income? The figure wasn't key; his relationship with money was. When I was called to board my plane I wasn't finished, so I scribbled, "Show me someone fifty-eight and spiritually awake." I shut my journal and got on the plane to Chicago.

At O'Hare, I was called to the airline counter. My seat had been changed to the middle seat of row eleven. As I settled in, an attractive man sat down in the aisle seat. We said hello and exchanged small talk. As the plane hit cruising altitude, he said, "I don't know how spiritually awake you are but . . ." I don't remember the rest. I was too stunned.

We talked nonstop to Tampa. We talked about our divorces, our families, our children, and our spiritual lives. I had to know his age. So I said something about my little brother and laughed, "Well, that's silly, he's fifty for heaven's sake."

The man asked, "How old are you?"

"Fifty-five."

"No way," he said, "I'm fifty-eight."

The rest of the flight was a haze. When we got to Tampa, he waited with me for my shuttle bus. He hugged me and asked me to call. I did. Three times. But with each call, more and more of the haze lifted. He wasn't at all what I wanted. Fifty-eight, yes. Spiritually awake, yes. But, truth be told, I wanted more—much, much more. It was time for the page.

Dear God,

I get it. I get that I can ask and receive. It was fun to ask for fifty-eight and spiritually awake and, voila, fifty-eight and spiritually awake sits down next to me. But I see now that this is not the best way to create my world. I won't treat the universe like my personal vending machine anymore. I'll have nice long chats with you first and seek your guidance and wisdom before I place any more requests.

I had long wrestled with the difference between goals and intentions. In my corporate life, we were forever prodded to set goals. So I set business goals. My self-help books preached the importance of personal goals. So I set personal goals. I met all my goals. But afterward, I always felt like saying, "So what?" Setting and meeting goals wasn't making me happy. Something was missing. The man in row eleven gave me a nice education on the difference between a goal and an intention. I had set a very specific goal grounded in details, and the universe had met that goal. But what I really wanted was a loving relationship, and neither age nor spiritual awareness could promise that.

In general, I've found that when I set a broader intention for a soul-satisfying outcome—in this case, a loving relationship—and leave the details of what, when, who, and how to Spirit, I end up receiving more than I can imagine. I see it as the difference between human mind and divine mind. Human mind sees an immediate need and begs for that. Divine mind sees the vast realm of possibility and creates a path to it all.

The First Wave: Intention

This week you will reach a deep understanding of what you truly want and why you want it. The next seven days will help you identify the goals, intentions, visions, and dreams that want to jump onto the heart-stirring picture of your joyous abundant life on your Intention Mandala. That life will come to pass, but in ways you can't currently predict. For today, send a Soul Slinky wave of intention as you step into this delightful week filled with creation toys. In seven days, you will send laughing waves of joy and gratitude right back.

the lotus and the lily

connect to power

We were created to be creators.

—John O'Donohue, *Beauty*

You've done a beautiful job of looking back, but now it's time to gently tuck the past into its bed, bless it, kiss it, and say goodnight. It's time to close that door and turn your face toward the rising dawn of your future. The next year of your life could be miraculous. It could be a year of wonder and joy. And you have the power to create it. Truth be told, like Dorothy in *The Wizard of Oz*, you've always had the power to return to your true home—your nature of shared divinity. But, if you're anything like me, you're just beginning to absorb that profound truth.

This week you're going to do some magical heel clicking. If you don't resonate with Dorothy's red shoes, select another symbol. At nine, my son fell in love with Harry Potter and his wand. On vacation, we found a store in Minneapolis that had a whole bucket full of wands. It took Jerry two hours of waving to select the perfect one. He's twenty-three now, but that wand still has a place of honor on his bookshelf and always will.

Here are a few power statements about your true nature as a spiritual being having a human experience. For fun, stand and click your heels or wave your wand as you say them. At first you may feel ridiculous, but stay with it. Speak them until you feel the power of the words come to life inside you.

Click

I am a spark of the Divine.

Click

I was created to create. I have the power to create.

Click

I believe. I believe in myself. I believe in my purpose. I believe in my potential. And I believe in my divine partner.

Click

I am unlimited.

Click

I am a miracle. My body is a miracle. My life is a miracle. My future is a miracle.

Click

I am the beloved of the Divine.

Click

I trust. I trust that I am loved, protected, guided, and led right into my abundant life.

These statements sound bold, but the vision of the mandala as a sphere tells us they're true. The black void holds everything in potential. Everything we want to create is there and is possible. And those slender gold threads deliver an endless supply of information. We are all connected to one another and to the whole. We are unlimited. Every one of these statements is actually true.

When I created my 2010 mandala, my friend Rev. Lauren McLaughlin gave me a little card with twelve affirmations and suggested I say them every day. Talk about power statements. It took me several months to get comfortable saying, "I am God's own perfect creation." (You can imagine what my inner critic had to say about that.) I didn't have quite so much trouble with "There is no other person on the planet exactly like me," but "Things always work out for me" felt presumptuous. But I kept saying them and slowly the words worked their way into my being. I think they moved into the vast, open spaces created by forgiveness and the demise of my thought worms. Those twelve affirmations worked real magic on me, moving me gently but irrevocably toward a new center, and in that center, I knew that I was "intimately connected to all the power of the universe."

That's the center you're going to stand in when you pray with your Intention Mandala every day. So step into that center now and try this affirmation on for size: *I am intimately connected to all the power of the universe.*

Say it. Let it sink in. It will start in your head as an idea—maybe even a fairly odd idea. Let the words drift down your throat, your heart, your solar plexus, your stomach, and into your gut. Let the words flow down your legs and out into the earth. Then draw the words back up into your feet from the blessed earth that sustains you. For fun, click your heels and say it again: *I am intimately connected to all the power of the universe.*

Then let the words flow back up through your chakras and out the top of your head, through your divine antenna, to connect with and attract the power of this beautiful universe—your true home. Now and forever, this is home. You belong here. You are one of its precious and powerful children—not a bad family to be a part of.

Till tomorrow, keep clicking!

Reflect

- Do I feel that, like Dorothy, I have the magical power to simply click my heels together and, poof, I'm home? Do I believe this power is possible for me?

- What is my concept of my divine home? How connected do I feel with this home?

- How do the power statements make me feel? Which ones made me whisper yes, and which ones made me wince?

Write

Dear Voice,

Well, today is fun, but also a bit unsettling. The kid in me loves the idea of magic, of just clicking my heels and voila! but the critical adult in me is telling me to stop this nonsense. That judgmental voice is whispering, "Who do you think you are?" So there's a part of me that isn't ready to play this game. I could tell that there was a problem when we got to "I am intimately connected to all the power of the universe." Do I really believe that? I mean, really? If I did, what would my life look like? If I really believed that, how would I act? It would be the end of whining, wouldn't it? The end of begging. The end of complaining. Oh my. You and I have lots to talk about today. So let's get started. Talk to me about this whole "intimately connected to all the power of the universe" thing. I'm ready to experience that. Show me how.

Explore

- Step into an imaginary circle of divine power. Click your heels or wave your wand and make your declarations. Play with the concept of being far more powerful than you realize.

- Write your own power statements. Don't be timid—write big truths. Step into your power circle and say them.

- Notice how you feel. Do you feel stronger? If not, what's keeping you from believing them?

Nourish

I am a powerful being with the power to create.

Want More?

Get Lauren McLaughlin's twelve affirmations at UnityNow: A Spiritual Awakening Center on the Internet (*youareawakening.com*).

Day 23

your foundation:
soul purpose

To be born is to be chosen. No one is here by accident. Each one of us was sent here for a special destiny.

—John O'Donohue, *Anam Cara*

In a few days, you will create an Intention Mandala with images of the experiences and joys you want in your life. Out of all the possibilities, how are you going to choose the few that are right for you? Logically, you might think step one is to make a nice long list. It's not. Step one is to find your unshakeable foundation. Without that foundation, your list has no center, no focus, no unifying force. Without that foundation, you don't really know what you want or what belongs in your life or on your mandala. And it's precisely this foundation that is often missing in our rush to ask and receive.

So begin by asking the foundation question, the most important question you can ask: what is my soul's purpose?

Don't know? Don't worry. Most of us don't. In our years and years of education, secular and spiritual, nobody asks us to name our purpose.

I lived a long time without a purpose. I'd been successful in three careers—teaching, recruiting, and consulting—but never felt a soul connection to my work. I worked for a paycheck, not a purpose. But heaven knew I longed for a purpose, something that would inspire me to leap out of bed with my heart on fire to fulfill it, and it sent help. On July 9, 1996, I was in a meeting with two other human resource consultants to diagnose a company's hiring problems. My friend Pat Akerberg walked in and said, "Put those folders away. We're going to do this instead" and held up *The Path* by Laurie Beth Jones. We listened as Pat read some questions from the book, and we wrote down our first thoughts. At the end, she told us to look at everything we'd written, circle the words we loved best, and turn those words into a sentence. I grabbed a blue index card and wrote, "Use words to connect people to the light." That sentence made no sense to me. It didn't appear to have anything to do with being a consultant who designs recruitment programs. I kept right on trying to build my consulting practice, but I held on to that card. Through three wrenching household moves, that blue card stayed with me. On some level, I must have known it was important.

My marriage blew up a few weeks after I wrote that card. Overnight life got scary. With nowhere to turn, I began to write long daily missives to "Dear God." Quickly, I discovered that I had access to wise counsel, loving comfort, and tangible help on the page. When the divorce finally ended, I began to teach deep soul writing. In 2006, Conari Press committed to publish *Writing Down Your Soul,* and my writing career began to blossom. But during all those years, I never thought about my blue card.

In the fall of 2007, as a part of my research for *Writing Down Your Soul,* I had my first Akashic Record reading. I asked the masters and teachers if I was fulfilling my soul's purpose. They said, "This is not the life you came in for, but when you checked the box, it brought forth all the talents that hadn't been developed. Writing is now your first and foremost purpose, and it will usher you out of this body."

After the reading, I frantically dug through my office closet. The blue card was right there waiting for me. I read it aloud: "Use words to connect people to the light." Oh my God! That's *exactly* what I do. I use words—written words, spoken words—to give people ways to connect to the light within. My soul knew the truth back in 1996, while my conscious self was busy trying to be a consultant.

When I made my first Intention Mandala, I pinned my blue soul-purpose card to the wall above it. Now I speak my soul purpose every day: "I, Janet Conner, commit today to use words to connect people to the Light." It feels so good to say my soul's delight out loud. And Spirit always sends the help I need to live it.

Would you like to know your soul's purpose? It's not difficult to find it. Your soul already knows. All you have to do is be still and give your soul space to speak. Use soul writing today to peek through that wide-open, round doorway that Rumi speaks of. Here are a few questions to explore, but don't stick with them. Let the conversation unfold naturally.

What did I love to do as a child?

What makes my heart sing?

Where do I find great meaning?

What are the most important things in my life?

Who am I when I am my whole, authentic, holy self?

Reflect

- What do I think a soul purpose is? A career? A feeling? A role?
- Have I ever searched for my soul purpose?
- Do I feel like I have a soul purpose?
- What would happen if I knew my soul's purpose?
- Do I want to know it? Or am I afraid it would change my life too much?

Write

Dear Voice,

This is exciting—and a little scary. Knowing my soul's purpose would change everything, wouldn't it? I can see that my purpose is my foundation, but I haven't stopped to consider it before asking for things or making decisions. But it makes so much sense. So let's begin. There are a few questions I'd like to explore with you, like that one about what I loved as a child. I've heard before that what you loved as a child is a clue to your purpose. So let's talk about this. What I loved, really loved, doing as a kid was . . .

Did you learn anything in your conversation with the Voice? Don't be concerned if a soul purpose didn't emerge. For now, just look at the words and circle the ones you like best. Do this quickly. Don't weigh the value of the words or how they might or might not fit a purpose statement. Just put on your nine-year-old's "This is fun" hat and circle any words that make your child-self smile.

Now write those words on slips of paper. Move them around. Let the words that want to go together move next to one another. If a word feels like it wants to be removed, take it off. Put the words in whatever order they seem to want to be in. Sit and look at the words. Do they have a message for you?

I know this process sounds ridiculously simple, but it works. It's organic. Instead of trying to manage the data with your conscious mind, you step back, observe the data, and let it tell you what it wants you to know.

I looked at my own soul-purpose statement to test this premise. Sure enough, my favorite words are there. *Words, connect, light*—these truly are my soul's favorite words. What are yours? And what are your favorite words telling you about your soul's desire?

If your soul purpose doesn't surface today, don't worry. It may emerge as the week goes by, or on your Soul Day, or later. Although it is lovely to have a soul statement that lifts your heart and lights your fire, it is not necessary right this moment. You can create a beautiful Intention Mandala without it. Because, in the end, we all have the same soul purpose: We are all here to experience love, give love, be love. We are here to know joy, and light the way to joy for others. Really—that's it.

Some of us fulfill this purpose one way, and others another. Some have a purpose that sounds like a profession, but most do not. Most sound like a state of being, an awareness, a gift. In *Blessings of the Cosmos,* Neil Douglas-Klotz describes our soul purpose as "more the feeling of being in rhythm with the cosmos, growing in the garden of life as a ripe plant, always evolving and changing."

Here are a few purpose statements from members of my soul-purpose discovery course, "Check the Box":

To be and express who I really am.

To live life fully.

To be a healer.

To express unconditional love.

To experience and model a life of intense joy.

These purposes sound simple, don't they? And they are. But when they came through, the person was overwhelmed with a feeling of joyful recognition bordering on ecstasy. It was as if their soul shouted, "Yes!" That's how you'll know you've got your soul purpose. Your heart will tell you, and there will be no doubt. But until your special message surfaces, you can have this one: to experience and share love and joy.

How does that feel?

Explore

- Play with any of these ideas and see what happens. If you perceive a soul-purpose statement, say thank you and write it down. Enjoy the feeling.
- If you don't receive a personal soul purpose, don't worry; for now, write one that exudes love and joy.

Nourish

My soul has a purpose.

Want More?

If you'd like to experience the full mystical journey to find your soul's unique and precious purpose, visit "Check the Box" on my website, *janetconnor.com*.

Day 24

ellen and your life around the corner

If the doors of perception were cleansed, everything would appear to man as it is, infinite.

—William Blake, *The Marriage of Heaven and Hell*

Jennifer Hill Robenalt, my heaven-sent publicist, sent an email one morning with strict orders: stop right now and watch Ellen DeGeneres's Tulane commencement address. I stopped working and watched. For the first four minutes, I laughed. This is Ellen, after all. But then, Ellen told a story about writing a letter to God. I burst into tears. Ellen DeGeneres found herself the same way I found myself—the same way you are finding yourself. Your self is right there inside of you—your vision, your purpose, your story, as it could be, as it will be.

In her speech, Ellen described herself living on a flea-infested mattress on the floor of a ratty apartment in New Orleans with no clue what to do with her life. She'd just learned that a good friend had died in a car accident. Ellen picked up a pen and poured out an angry, hurt, confused letter to God. She asked big questions: Why is she gone, and I'm still here? What's my purpose?

As the words tumbled out, Ellen found Ellen—the real Ellen, the big Ellen, the potential Ellen. At the time she wrote that letter, she wasn't doing standup comedy, yet she wrote that she was going to be the first female comedian in history to be called over to sit across from Johnny Carson after doing her standup act on the show. Given her situation that was absurd. But guess what? Ellen was not only the first; she was the only woman to sit in that spot.

Ellen's vision really struck me. I wanted to see my big, potential, future self, too. Who wouldn't? The next morning, standing at my altar, I closed my eyes and had a little chat with Spirit. As I began to talk about Ellen's experience, I saw in my mind a white, glowing light about the size of a basketball. Instinctively, I looked into the white ball. As I did, I said aloud, "Now I'm going to have my own conversation with God and see my future." I sat down and asked on the page, "What is in my life around the corner?" Out gushed two pages of things, among them talking to Ellen about her letter to God, being interviewed by Robin Roberts on *Good Morning America*, speaking in front of a huge audience, and seeing my name on a *New York Times* list of bestselling authors.

I looked at all the delightful possibilities and wrote, "I love them all, but what one experience will be proof that all this has transpired and more? What *one* experience sums up my life around the corner? Instantly I knew. I drew a bold blue ink circle around these words: "I walk into the New York City main library with Jerry. He's an adult. We walk up to a shelf full of books, stop, and stare at them. I reach out and slowly run my hand along a dozen or more with my name on the spine. I start to cry. Jerry touches my arm, pulls me close, and says, 'Well, done, Mum. Well done.'"

Even as I type that sentence, I feel tears. Tears are proof that this is the apex experience I will have. I don't know when. When is not my job. I don't know how. How is not my job. I just know it *will* happen. I am standing there right now, in my white ball of light, smiling, and running my fingers slowly along all the books I have written. I turn to Jerry and with tears in my eyes and say, "Here I am, and here I'll be, even after I die. In the New York City Library. Guarded by lions."

Now it's your turn.

Close your eyes. Hold a white ball of divine light and peer into it. Ask your loving divine partner, "What happens in my life around the corner?" Then pick up a pen and start writing—*fast*. Watch as the images pour through you onto the page. No matter how wacky or amazing or unlikely or impossible, write them down. Why? Because Ellen sat next to Johnny Carson. And I will run my hands over my books in the main library in New York. That's why.

Now, what do you see?

Reflect

- What do I feel about Ellen's story?
- Do I think it's possible to see the future? Do I think it's possible for me?
- Am I ready to look into that white ball of light? Am I willing to try? Am I willing to suspend reality and believe, if just for a moment, so I can see my future?

Write

Dear Voice,

Okay, I'll play. You hand me a glowing ball of light, and I'll look inside. I can do that. When I look inside, I will be able to see what you see—the life I'm here to live, the life of divine purpose, the life I'm helping to create. Okay, I'm looking. Here's what I see . . .

Explore

- Watch Ellen's 2009 Tulane commencement address on YouTube.

- Do the life-around-the-corner experiment. Look into the glowing white light. Write down everything you see—quickly and with no conscious thought and no judgment of any kind. Just allow the images to come.

- Out of everything that pours onto the page, pick one that is the culmination, the proof that you are living your life of purpose and joy. Feel the scene. See the place, notice the people, smell the air, feel the weather. Who's there? What do they say? What are you doing? How do you feel?

- Draw a little picture of your life-around-the-corner scene or write a description on a card. Put your card on your altar or nightstand or somewhere special where you'll see it often.

- Visit your life around the corner often. It is just around the corner, and next week when you create your Intention Mandala, you will take a big step toward bringing it to life.

Nourish

I see my beautiful future.

Want More?

Read something that helps you see differently. One poet who helps me see what is right in front of me with brand new eyes is Mary Oliver. If you are not familiar with her poetry, start with her encounter with a grasshopper in "The Summer Day" (*The Truro Bear and Other Adventures*).

Day 25

the trust thermometer

In truth I tell you, if you have faith and do not doubt at all, not only will you do what I have done to the fig tree, but even if you say to this mountain, "Be pulled up and thrown into the sea," it will be done. And if you have faith, everything you ask for in prayer, you will receive.

—Jesus, Matthew 21:22 (The New Jerusalem Bible)

There's one problem with this delightful week of getting clear about all the wonderful things you want. And if you don't acknowledge that problem, if you don't give it room to express itself, if you don't stop and listen to it, it won't just meander away. Oh no. It will lie in wait and snap its fangs when you're feeling weak and vulnerable. With your defenses down, this monster can and will derail any project, any dream, any desire for a more beautiful, more abundant life. That problem is trust. In fact, it's the primary problem we all have. Do you have issues with trust? Try these questions on for size and see what your stomach tells you:

> Do I deeply trust that the universe supports me? Or do I sense that it punishes or thwarts me?

> Do I trust that I am always guided and protected? Or do I feel alone sometimes?

> Do I trust that I have a loving divine partner? And my partner wants only peace, joy, and abundance for me?

Do I trust that prayer works? That my prayers work? That my prayers work all the time?

Do I believe that I can change my life? Or do I feel trapped by circumstances or people?

Now what do you think? Got a few trust issues? Don't be surprised. Everyone does. The question isn't whether or not you have trust issues; it's how can you move through them. How can you reach that state where you know, and you know that you know, that you are always protected, always guided, always led?

I asked my Voice about this. Well, actually, I didn't *ask*. I whined. I moaned. I cried. My situation looked and felt perilous at the time, and I didn't feel Spirit was at hand or that all was well. "What's wrong with me?" I begged. "Why am I constantly returning to this place of panic? Why don't I feel safe? Why don't I—can't I—trust that you are here with me and it's all going to be all right?" Here's what I was told:

Trust is a movement, like increments on a thermometer. When you are locked in the state of *doubt*, the trust thermometer registers cold.

When you take a baby step from doubt into a willingness to *suspend disbelief*, the temperature moves up to cool. The willingness to suspend disbelief is like the predawn glow. It's not exactly light, but it's not black either. Once you suspend disbelief, things really start moving.

When you step into a state of *hope*, of possibility, the temperature moves up to almost warm.

When you place a request for guidance or a little miracle and it comes to pass, you are surprised perhaps, but excited, and the temperature rises to warm. You are now in *tested trust*.

I've been in the state of tested trust for years. It started in the throes of my divorce. One day in desperation, I wrote, "I don't know how you're going to do it, but I know that you are. Thank you in advance for $10,000 for the attorney." Two days later I had $10,000. I was stunned. So I tested again. And, oh my goodness, it worked again! And again. I received everything I asked for, sometimes within hours.

The next step up from tested trust is *unshakable trust*. Let's say tested trust is seventy degrees and unshakable trust is seventy-eight degrees. They sound pretty close, don't they? But as I discovered, moving from tested trust to unshakable trust doesn't feel like just a few degrees of improvement; it feels like a logarithmic leap, a giant jump over a chasm—a chasm so wide you can't even see the other side. What I wanted to know—what I *needed* to know—is how do I make the giant leap from tested trust to unshakable trust? If I could just figure out what the in-between step was, I could take it and get across that gap.

I asked on the page, and nothing showed up. So I scheduled an angel reading with Margo Mastromarchi. I asked, "How do I get from tested trust to unshakable trust?"

There was a long pause; then the answer came: "One word," the angels said, *"Decide."*

Decide? That's it? My brain was so disappointed. It wanted a step, an action, a how-to, but my heart thumped in agreement. How could there be a safe, slow, methodical, step-by-step way to enter into a complete state of trust? I'd had my baby steps, my trial period of tested trust, and I'd been dabbling in it for years. Now it was time to just close my eyes and leap, knowing that the universe is safe, knowing that I am guided and loved, knowing that I have a divine purpose, knowing that Spirit protects me, and knowing that miracles can and do happen—and they can and do happen to me.

Decide. See the chasm and leap anyway. See the potential; see your life around the corner, and start living like it's going to happen. Feel the joy of unshakeable trust even before you see the proof. Joy first, miracles second.

Paradox Alert:
The path to trust is trust.

Are you in that space between tested trust and unshakeable trust? I have some good news if you are. It's not an unfathomable chasm, and crossing into unshakeable trust requires only a tiny, one-word, one-moment, one-breath move. Say yes. Say

Yes, I believe. Yes, I trust Spirit. Yes, I want to break through to a new kind of divinely guided, joy-filled life. Yes, to my soul's purpose. Yes, I embrace my divinely guided future. I say yes to it all—whenever and however it is meant to unfold.

Yes, I decide. I choose. I declare that I am the creator of a beautiful life. And really what is there to be afraid of? I don't have to do this alone; I have a partner—a *divine* partner for heaven's sake. So is this really all that scary?

Today, this moment, this second, decide.

Reflect

- Is trust an issue for me?
- Do these five stages of trust make sense? How do I measure trust?
- What is my current reading on the trust thermometer?
- Is the only way to experience trust to decide to trust? If so, how do I feel about that?

- Do I want to decide to live in a state of real unshakeable trust? If so, what am I going to do? When am I going to decide?
- How will I know I've made the decision?

Write

Dear Voice,

We've never talked about trust before. Isn't that odd? I mean, really, here I am talking with you every day, and I've never said whether I trust you. And not just you—the whole universe. Come on, a lot of crummy things have happened, and I sure didn't feel safe when they did. So why should I trust that all is well? Before I go deciding anything, you and I need to have a long talk. What is trust? Where am I on this trust thermometer? And furthermore, how am I going to have more trust? Janet gave us this thermometer thing, but I want to hear it from you. What do I need to know about trust right now?

Explore

- Draw a picture of the thermometer or design your own symbol. Do the stages fit, or have you experienced other shades of doubt and trust? What's your overall picture of your relationship with trust?
- Mark where you are in your current relationship with trust and where you want to be.
- Decide to make the leap.
- Pay attention to what happens after you decide. Collect evidence of the universe's response to your decision. Is it the "uh-oh!" response or something delightful? Or both?
- Pay attention to your dreams.
- Contemplate the temperature in the state beyond unshakeable trust—communion. This is where the

masters and mystics live. As Jesus said, "The Father and I are one."

Nourish

I decide to trust.

Want More?

Spend some time with *Meditations with Meister Eckhart* by Matthew Fox. The poems are short and sweet, yet somehow they are all deep treatises on the power and joy of divine trust.

Day 26

fill your cart

Your father knows what you need before you ask.

—Jesus, Matthew 6:8
(Holy Bible from the Ancient Eastern Text)

Today is the delightful day when you fill your cart with all the goodies you want in your beautiful life.

When you began the Lotus and the Lily process, you might have thought that the idea was to get clear about what you want, ask for it, and then stand back and receive. Yes, that is what we're doing, but we're doing it in a much deeper, more soul-directed way. We're asking the way Jesus taught two thousand years ago, in a famous passage that is usually translated as "Ask and it shall be given to you, seek and ye shall find, knock and it shall be opened" (Matthew 7:7). But Jesus had more to say than the modern usage of the word *ask* conveys. We have taken ask to mean request something we want. That, according to Meister Eckhart, is treating God like a cow.

Some people, I swear,
>   want to love God in the same way as they love a cow.
>   They love it for its milk and cheese and the profit
>   they can derive from it.

—from *Meditations with Meister Eckhart*, Matthew Fox

In Aramaic, Jesus did not say walk up to the cow and ask for what you want. As Neil Douglas-Klotz explains in *Blessings of the Cosmos*, his retranslation of Jesus's original Aramaic words, what Jesus actually said in Matthew 7:7 was,

> Ask intensely—
>> like a straight line engraved toward
>> the object you want;
>
> pray with desire—
>> as though you interrogated your own soul about
>> its deepest, most hidden longings;
>
> and you will
>
> receive expansively—
>> not only what your desire asked,
>> but where the elemental breath led you—
>> love's doorstep, the place where you
>
> bear fruit
>> and become part of the universe's
>> power of generation and sympathy.
>
> Search anxiously—
>> from the interior of your desire
>> to its outer embodiment—

With these criteria—interrogating your soul, following the path to love, and searching from inside your desires—the items you put in your cart today are probably quite different from those you might have chosen a month ago. If, back on Day 1, you'd made a mandala of the things you wanted, you would have created a life, but it might not have been the life your soul wants. It might not have been the life your angels and guides are joyfully waiting to help you create. It might not have been the life that supports your soul's purpose or moves you toward your life around the corner. Thanks to all your deep explorations in the last twenty-five days, you now know how to interrogate your soul to sift and winnow your list down to what you really, really want.

Begin by making an unedited list. Just like a kid getting ready for a birthday or holiday, jot down anything and everything you want. Don't pick or choose yet and don't judge any of your choices; just get them all on paper.

Now, look at what you've written and start interrogating your soul. Ask what lies behind each item. Remember that pile of money on Day 15? It isn't the money we want; it's the freedom we can create with the money. Same with health. Let's say you want to lose weight. What freedom lies within a healthier, lighter body? Or releasing addiction? Or becoming debt free? Or having a baby? Or meeting your true love? Or changing careers? Or writing a book? What soul-expanding, life-affirming truth lies beneath each desire?

As you look deep within each item, you may find you want to rename or reframe some items. Several may be pointing toward the same freedom and can be merged. Others may simply fall off the list.

When you take something off your list, please don't think that means you can't or won't have it. When I made my first Intention Mandala, I didn't draw a car. It just didn't feel all that important in comparison to the things my soul deeply wanted like my perfect agent, book publisher, and joyous work. But six months later, a sapphire blue sedan was in my driveway. Why? Because my divine guides knew my old car was no longer safe. If your divine guides know you need things you've taken off your list, they'll see that those things are "added unto you."

At this point, you probably still have a pretty long list. There is no correct number, but most people put eight to twelve items on their Intention Mandala. Fewer than six sounds like you don't trust that the universe is generous or that you deserve a truly abundant life. More than twelve sounds like you don't trust the universe to notice and take care of you unless you dictate everything in advance.

The following questions may help you interrogate your soul about your desires. If, as you explore them on the page or in meditation, your soul responds with a big, yelping yes, that item belongs in your new abundant life and on your Intention Mandala. As always, these questions are just suggestions. To create your own soul-interrogation questions, go back to your most significant experiences in this program and, in light of the wisdom those experiences unearthed for you, craft new questions or criteria that can help you explore the interior of your desires.

Is this item what my waves of intention and gratitude have been leading me toward?

Will it help me stay awake?

Does this support my feeling of being enough?

Does this keep me away from my old movie and thought worms?

Is this worth my universe cash?

Does this support my soul's purpose or take me into a deeper experience of love and joy?

Does this match my power statements?

Would my GrandSelf select this?

Does this item move me toward my life around the corner?

Are my angels and guides affirming this for me?

Does this item make my heart leap and my soul sing?

Are these the seeds I want to see grow in my life?

Taken as a whole, does this collection of items form a cohesive picture of my beautiful, abundant life?

In the end, the real question is simply, does my soul want this? Taken collectively, do the items on your list describe the life your soul wants to create? I can't answer that question for you. No one can. And don't let anyone tell you what belongs on your Intention Mandala. It's your life, your soul, your cart. Only you can decide what goes in it.

By the time you've finished interrogating your soul, you will probably have a list with ten or so desires. Don't fret about whether or not they are the final items that will go on your mandala. You're going to review everything on your Soul Day after you identify your conditions. The conditions will help you solidify what you want. For now, just put all the items in your cart.

And speaking of that cart, do you know what your cart looks like? Last April, a group of soul writers and I explored the beauty of Mother Earth in Costa Rica. Our last stop on our last day was the town of Sarchi, home of the famous Costa Rican decorated oxcarts. When oxcarts were the primary mode of transportation, families painted their oxcarts with elaborate designs that identified their farm. Some of those families still produce and decorate oxcarts, only now those carts are objets d'art, not farm equipment.

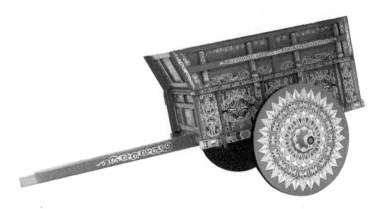

Photo by Gayle Lawrence, Journeys of Discovery

Whenever I think about filling my cart with all the delightful things I want, I picture one of these colorful oxcarts with my own personal soul crest. I visualize it pulled not by an ox, but by a beautiful horse. The horse represents Spirit, the One, the creative force at the center of my mandala and the universe.

Your cart doesn't have to be a Costa Rican oxcart. Perhaps it's an ornate Victorian sleigh or the bed of a four-wheel truck or a tender pulled behind a sailboat. For Linda Bryant in Nashville, it's a hay cart. In her life around the corner, Linda saw herself in a sunlit hayloft. She doesn't yet know the full meaning of that image, but to help it come to life, she decided her cart should contain a bed of golden hay.

The image of your cart doesn't matter; choose whatever makes you happy and sings the song of your abundant life. Then fill it in joy.

Reflect

- Have I been treating God like a cow?
- What does my cart look like?
- What do I want in my cart?
- How many items do I want in my cart? What does the number tell me?
- What are my criteria for deciding what to put in and what to leave out?
- How can I interrogate my soul to create a list for my mandala?

Write

Dear Voice,

I think I'm finally getting the hang of how to ask in this way—not the milk-and-cheese way, but the soul-interrogation way. But I'm not absolutely sure, so let's do this together. Let's start with a giant wish list . . .

Okay, now help me look at each item and see what's behind it . . . Oh! A few surprises here. I see several that don't really belong in my cart.

Now help me with the soul-interrogation piece. The biggest ahas in this program have been the thought worms, my old movie title, not feeling good enough, and . . . From those, let's come up with criteria to use as measuring sticks for what I want . . .

Oh my! My list really is changing. I am surprised. I thought I knew what I wanted, but this is a deeper way of getting clear about that. I really am praying and searching intensely. And I think I'm getting closer to what my soul really wants . . .

Okay, here's our list. I like it. For now, let's put these in the cart. Hey, what's the cart? Janet's oxcart is cute, but my cart is a . . .

Explore

- Make and edit your list using my suggested soul-interrogation questions or anything that will help you identify what you want in your beautiful, abundant life.
- Design your cart. It can be just in your mind, or you might enjoy drawing it or finding an image online.
- Fill your cart.

Nourish

I fill my cart with the desires of my soul.

Want More?

Read *Blessings of the Cosmos* by Neil Douglas-Klotz.

Day 27

name your year

Any word spoken with clear realization and deep concentration has a materializing value.

—Paramahansa Yogananda, *Autobiography of a Yogi*

In Week 2, "Look Back," you named the movie of your past. Now you get to name the movie of your future—your forthcoming year. I've named my year four times now, and each time, I think I know what I'm doing. (Hear that giggling? It's my angels.) I imagine all the lovely things my newborn year will bring, and I give my year a delightful name that somehow captures all that.

But twelve months later, I invariably discover that when I put the name of my year on my Intention Mandala, I did not fully understand what I was declaring. Mind you, it's not that I'm unhappy. I'm always delighted with the results. But the name is often a comical comparison of the small size of my vision and the big size of Spirit's.

On January 1, 2011, I had a lovely Soul Day filled with rich conversations with my Voice. We looked back over all the gifts and learning of 2010 and forward to my dreams for 2011. I thought I had a name picked out, but the morning of my Soul Day I woke with "Big Pot" in my head. I didn't understand it at the time, but the next day, when I looked at the mandala I'd made, I realized I'd unconsciously drawn the cook's view of my orange Le Creuset dutch oven. Throughout the holidays, I'd stood over that pot for hours on end, trying to make an authentic ragu bolognese. When I realized that my hours of stirring had somehow worked their way onto my mandala, I laughed, and I added little orange handles to my mandala. Then I cut a four-inch pot out of orange construction paper, poked a slit in it, and stuck in a brown paper spoon. I wrote "2011 Big Pot" on it and taped it to the bottom of my mandala. I joked aloud, "I think this means you're the chef and I'm the ragu. Go ahead. Start stirring me into something delicious." I did not realize at the time just how powerful a prayer the name "Big Pot" was. In two words, I gave up control and stepped all the way into surrender. And surrender, I promise you, is one amazing recipe for success. Did the name make a difference? Well, here's what came to pass in 2011. See what you think.

January: I created my "Your Soul Wants Five Things" learning series.

February: I was a faculty member on an educational cruise, and I held my first big name teleseminar.

March: I taught the Lotus and the Lily weekend intensive for the first time, and I signed with my literary agent.

April: I led a soul venture to Costa Rica.

May: I taught the course "Writing Down Your Soul."

June: I taught the course "Soul Vows," and I created a soul-writing program for women for the police department.

July: I designed a brand new soul purpose course called "Check the Box."

August: I gave a new talk, "The Connection Is in Your Hands."

September: I designed a new course, "Plug In for Expressive Souls" and taught another called "Plug In for Writers."

October: I led the first "How to Become a Container for Miracles" weekend intensive experience and finished the book proposal for *The Lotus and the Lily*.

November: I taught "The Lotus and the Lily" telecourse and signed a publishing contract for the book.

December: I completed the manuscript for *The Lotus and the Lily*.

There's no doubt in my mind that naming 2011 "Big Pot" helped materialize this delicious stew of rewards, joys, friendships, synchronicities, income, and more. Spirit makes a fine ragu, I must say!

Alice Manning named her 2011 "Wild Horses Couldn't Drag Me Away from My Divine Purpose." In November, she realized what the name actually meant.

When I wrote that name, I was thinking of my divine purpose as something that was going to be added and nothing could drag me from that new identity. But what's really gone on this year is a continuous shedding of all identities and becoming keenly aware that my craving for identity, for purpose—divine or otherwise—was fueled in part by ego's desire to be somebody, to be validated. When I think of those wild horses today, I see them as all my ego's plans for validation trying to drag me into another graduate program or something to legitimize myself. I have not let those wild horses drag me away from my core work of being, knowing, opening to the mystery and power of what is, and trusting what emerges organically from that place. And this, in itself, could be the fulfillment of my divine purpose— or maybe, more accurately, the achievement of the state from which that purpose will spring, in divine timing.

The moral of these stories is that you actually don't know what the name of your year means—not at the human conscious level. But your soul does. It's your higher self, your divine self, your GrandSelf that chooses the name. So just let it happen. Let a title come to you. Twelve months from now, you will find out what it means.

Reflect

- Do I think a name, a few words, has actual power to materialize?

- What did I name my old movie? Does the name of my past movie hold clues to the name of my coming year?

- If I wanted to name my coming year, what words spring immediately to mind?

Write

Dear Voice,

This is a fun idea. If I can stare into a crystal ball and imagine my future, I can surely play with the idea of naming the next twelve months. Okay, let's play. If my year is to be truly one of purpose and joy, if my year is to help bring my soul's purpose to life, if I really am building an abundant life with you, my divine partner, what will it look like?

What words capture that vision? Give me some ideas here for the perfect name for my future—a name that lifts my heart, excites me, makes me smile. Give me a name for my year of abundance, purpose, and joy.

Explore

- Play with the idea of a name for next year. It may come quickly on the page or in your mind, but if it doesn't, don't worry. There are many ways it can come to you.

- As you're falling asleep, ask for the perfect name for your coming year. Then, when you wake, lie still for a while and allow images from your dreams to come back to you.

- The perfect name may come while you're driving, making dinner, walking, or doing some other every-day activity. Just set the intention to find the name, and your guides will take it from there. All you have to do is pay attention.

- If you get a name, write it down. Look at it for a few days. If it's the right one, you'll know. You won't be able to keep a smile off your face.

- If you don't get a name, don't worry. It will come. Perhaps it will come at the last moment as you are completing your Intention Mandala.

Nourish

I name my future.

Want More?

Read *Autobiography of a Yogi* by Paramahansa Yogananda. Some of the clearest and wisest interpretations of the sayings of Jesus are in the footnotes.

Day 28

focus only on
what's coming in

There is an uncanny symmetry between the inner and outer world. Each person is the sole inhabitant of their own inner world; no-one else can get in there to configure how things are seen. Each of us is responsible for how we see, and how we see determines what we see.

—John O'Donohue, *Beauty*

This week has been fun, hasn't it? You now have heel-clicking power statements, the strong foundation of your soul's purpose, a startling view from your life around the corner, a whole new relationship with trust, and a cartful of dreams. You might even have a name for your coming year. If all that hasn't fallen into place, don't worry. You will review all of it and more on your Soul Day. No matter where you are, stop for a moment and imagine all kinds of good things coming to you. See them. I mean that literally: actually see your good flying through the air, coming through your window, and landing in your hands.

On December 27, 2009, I learned how important seeing is. I was exactly where you are. I had spent twenty-seven days slogging through some rather deep spiritual woods, and although I loved all I'd done and all I'd learned, I sensed something was missing, because I was still broke and still scared about declaring bankruptcy. So I scheduled an angel reading and asked the angels what to do about my financial situation. They said:

Do not focus on what is going out. Focus *only* on what is coming in, and it will multiply. You are the only reason you do not see it coming. See it. See it as checks, checkbooks, bank accounts, receipts of paid bills. See only that. And as you see it, open your hands.

The angels were right. For months my eyes had been riveted only on what was going out. I'd write lists of bills and their due dates. I'd go to bed worried about bills and wake in the morning with images of bills in my head. I'd go to my desk and jockey funds around to make sure I had just enough money in the right account on the right day. The only thing in my mind was money going out.

I hung up the phone and went straight to my writing chair. In my mind, I imagined everything I wanted: my next telecourse filled to capacity, a juicy royalty check, new speaking invitations, unexpected income falling out of the sky. As I was seeing all this good, a power bill snuck in and grabbed my attention. I swatted it away and shifted my focus back to what I wanted to come in. I saw money flying through my office window. I stayed with that image until I felt it land on my chest. I saw my business bank statement with a ten thousand dollar balance float through the window and settle in my hands. I sat there until I could *see* everything I wanted coming to me.

The next morning, I woke in a panic as the mortgage statement poked me in the eye. I turned my face to the window. It was a glorious sunny morning. I forced myself to see my good riding through the glass on sunbeams. I stayed there until I saw a lovely wad of money coming through the window. I waited until I felt it land with a plop on my chest. Plop. Plop. Plop. Laughing, I got out of bed, opened the curtain, and called out, "This is the day the Lord has made. I am grateful and rejoice in it" (Psalms 118:24). That felt so good, I've said it every morning since.

The next morning, however, the bills were right there in their standard starting position, expecting me to worry about them. I blinked and looked at the window instead. I stayed there until I could see good things riding on the sunlight to me. During the day, as soon as I felt panic, I'd stop and stare at a window and see something good coming to me. And when I paid a bill, I made myself smile and say aloud, "I am grateful to be able to pay this bill." It took several weeks, but eventually bill paying became a pleasant, prayer-filled activity.

It's your turn to play this game. Visualize what you want. See your good and *only* your good, in all its delightful forms. See it moving through the air and seeking you. Watch it fly into your checking account, pantry, driveway, home, calendar, and heart. Feel it land on your body. Listen to the angels' instructions one more time and take these words to heart:

See what you want to see. See it coming. See only that.

See the flow, and as you see it, open your hands.

Reflect

- Where has my attention been? What have I been seeing?
- What do I want to see?
- How would it feel to see what I want landing on me?
- What would my life look like if my eyes were locked only on all the gifts of Spirit?

Write

Dear Voice,

Oh boy, this is so true. I've been looking so often and so hard at my problems that they've grabbed most of my attention. I get this. I need to shift my eyes onto the life I want. With your help, I can see only my good. Talk to me. Show me. Guide me. Teach me. How do I keep my eyes only on your gifts?

Explore

- Notice your first thoughts as you wake. Catch any negative or scary thoughts and substitute thoughts that remind you that you are safe and connected with Spirit and all is well.

- Lie in bed and see wonderful things coming to you. See them and feel them touch you. Smile when you get out of bed.

- Listen to the first words you say in the morning. Do you want to say something heart lifting, like Psalm 118:24? Find or write something short and delightful. Then say it for a week and notice how you feel.

- The masters and teachers of the Akashic Record told me something that fits today perfectly: "You cannot create the next moment out of frustration with the moment that is. Therefore, the moment that is before you is filled with beauty." Find the beauty in your moment, especially your fearful moments, and everything will change.

- Observe how you talk to yourself. Substitute language that isn't fear based.

- When you go somewhere that has been a source of pain, like a doctor's office, bless all the people who work there and see them helping you.

Nourish

I focus only on what's coming in.

Want More?

Read how John O'Donohue talks about vision in *Beauty*. It will change the way you see forever.

The Second Wave: Gratitude

What a week of divine play this has been! Are you feeling gratitude and joy for the beautiful ideas that have come your way? Then hold your Soul Slinky in your hands and send waves of gratitude back to the intention you set at the beginning of this week. While you're at it, send waves of gratitude to yourself, your guides, your angels, your divine partner—everyone and everything that helped bring you to this place.

You are now ready for your Soul Day and Intention Mandala. And that is worthy of celebration. You created a beautiful preparation. You looked back with love at your life to date. You untied many, many knots of unforgiveness and, in the process, created massive amounts of space for your new abundant life. And you've filled your cart with beautiful things for your new, abundant life. You've nourished twenty-eight sections of your spiritual fields. Celebrate!

Day 29

soul-day preparation

A day of Silence
Can be a pilgrimage in itself.

A day of Silence
Can help you listen
To the Soul play
Its marvelous lute and drum.

—Hafiz, from "Silence," *I Heard God Laughing,*
Translation by Daniel Ladinsky

Congratulations! You are now ready to create your beautiful day of pilgrimage, your Soul Day. You may want more than one day to prepare. You may also find that you'd like to divide your Soul Day into parts, setting aside two half days or perhaps several evenings. Or you may decide to hold your Soul Day in a retreatlike manner, celebrating it over one or two whole days. I set aside all of January 1 for my Soul Day and a few hours on January 2 to finish my mandala. But you can have your Soul Day any time you want. For many, the busy holidays don't leave enough time for undertaking all the Lotus and the Lily activities, so they wait until Epiphany, the twelfth day after Christmas, to hold their Soul Day. Others give themselves a Soul Day on their birthday. Choose any date you want.

Glance through the steps suggested here and plan your special day. Incorporate any activities that help you connect with your beloved Divine: sacred reading, yoga, meditation, prayer, long walks, even a nap. If you're uncertain what to do, ask your angels and guides for help. But don't feel that you have to know exactly what you are going to do in advance. Just show up with the intention of being open and available, and everything will unfold. There may be surprises in store—in fact, I guarantee it. There will be surprises—delicious, divine surprises. Let them come.

Set Up Sacred Space

1. Decide where you'll have your Soul Day. Will it be where you do your deep soul writing, or do you feel called to be somewhere else?

2. Look at the space. Do you want to remove any clutter? Do you have a comfortable place to write? Is there enough light? Is it quiet? Is there room to create your mandala? Does the space feel holy? Are there any sacred objects you'd like to add? Choose something special to mark the place and honor the experience that will happen there. Look around for a special talisman to bless you on your day of soul.

3. Set up everything in advance. Here are a few things to consider having in your space:

   - Scents. Set up candles, oils, flowers—something to activate the sense of smell. If you want the scent of lilies, get them a couple days before your Soul Day so they are open and fragrant.

   - Books. Gather your sacred texts, mystical poetry, *You Are Here, Blessings of the Cosmos,* or any other books calling to you right now.

   - Journal. Place your deep-soul-writing journal and pen next to your writing chair.

   - Sound. Set up your favorite sacred music or other sound that will lift and support you during this sacred experience. This might be a lovely day to play any of Deva Premal's CDs, the *Theta Music* CD that I have for sale on my website, or perhaps *The Ghandarva Experience,* a CD by Tom Kenyon. If you feel led to give yourself the gift of silence, follow that urge.

- Flower essences. Green Hope Farms has created a flower essence especially to support those doing the Lotus and the Lily program; it's called "the Lotus and the Lily," and you can order it online at *greenhopeessences.com.* Or you can get a Bach flower essence from your local health food store.

- Water glass and pitcher. You'll be doing a lot of deep soul writing and drinking a lot of water. It might be fun to drink out of a special glass on your Soul Day.

- Holy oils or water. If you have sacred oils or water, this would be a lovely time to use them. You can bless your own. I have a tiny vial of Sai Baba's vibhuti (holy ash), and I rub a bit on my hands before I make my mandala.

- Food. You'll stop to eat, but perhaps you'd like fruit or other beautiful food in the room. The more senses that are engaged, the better.

- Final blessing materials. Gather your favorite oracle cards or anything you'd like to use for a special blessing at the end.

4. Gather your mandala-construction materials.

- Get a pad of 11 x 17 sketch paper (a nice size and easy to find) or a few poster-board sheets in colors you like. Buy a bit more than you expect to use. If you want to make a spinning mandala, get something stiff.

- If you are making a mandala that spins, get a piece of foam board or something to pin it to. Then find a special pin for the center. The pin represents Spirit, the unifying force of the universe, and allows the pieces of the mandala to move. Depending on how thick your mandala and backing are, a long pushpin, sewing pin, or tack might do the trick. Tie tacks or post earrings work well because they are short and clasp tightly in the backing.

- A compass will allow you to draw circles, or you can create circles by tracing plates.

- Gather colored pencils, markers, or any other drawing utensils you'd like to use to decorate your mandala.

- If you want to paste pictures on your mandala, collect magazines or other images.

- Don't forget scissors, pencils, glue, and tape, and long pushpins or other means of attaching the finished mandala to the wall.

Give Yourself the Gift of a Full Stop

Honor yourself and the life you are here to live by setting aside time to design it and nurture it. Time is the one gift you can give yourself. Give it. Honor yourself with the gift of a Soul Day. Don't say you will do your Soul Day when there's time. Mark it on your calendar—now.

Your Soul Day is special. It's a rare opportunity to withdraw from daily life and "listen to your soul play its marvelous lute and drum," as Hafiz says. So create a space and time where your soul can speak at length. Because electronic media segment your consciousness and distract your brain, turn off the phone, computer, and TV. Give yourself the gift of being fully and completely present to yourself, your soul, and the Divine.

Prepare Your People

Ask the people you live with for the gift of silence, space, and privacy. If others in your home have been doing the Lotus and the Lily program and want to have a Soul Day on the same day, consider working in separate rooms or not sharing your mandalas until the process is complete. Couples tell me that this is such a private, soul-centered experience that the presence of someone else in the room, no matter how much you love him or her, can be a distraction. Plus, we are so conditioned to adjust our preferences to meet the needs of those we love that it can be easy to slip into creating a mandala that describes the life someone else wants. This day is about connecting with Source to discern the life your soul wants to create.

Children love to make mandalas. A shared Soul Day can be a truly special family tradition and an amazing way to cap off the holidays or honor a child's birthday or other important event. Some families make one mandala that holds the intentions of the whole family. Others make individual mandalas. For a group mandala event, set out a lot of construction materials and pictures and explain the process in a simple way.

Ask for Guidance

As you fall asleep the night before, ask for any last guidance. Place a notepad on your nightstand. If possible, don't set an alarm. Allow yourself to wake naturally so you can take full advantage of the rich morning theta brain-wave state between sleep and full wakefulness.

During the night, if a word or phrase pushes you toward wakefulness, roll over and write what you hear on your notepad. Do not turn on the light or sit up unless you feel so much coming through that you simply have to sit up to capture it all. After you've jotted what you heard, whisper thank you, place your pen below what you've written (you might be awakened with more), and go back to sleep.

Reflect

- How do I feel about creating my Soul Day? Do I feel ready?
- Where do I want to have my Soul Day? How can I make the space ready?
- When am I going to hold my Soul Day?
- Are the people around me supportive? What do I need or want from them?
- What last piece of guidance do I want?

Write

Dear Voice,

Well, here we are at the conclusion of a month of amazing soul adventures. You and I have had so many important conversations. Now it's time to bring it all to life. I think I'm ready. Am I? We've covered a lot of ground, but I still wonder if I have the ability to create my life. That still seems so big. I'm excited, but a bit nervous too. What's going to happen? Where will I be in a year? Help me get confident about this, and help me get ready.

Explore

- Get the materials for your mandala.
- Decide where you will have your Soul Day.
- Gather everything you want in your space. Set the stage. Bless it and then be at peace that everything will unfold as it should.
- Set aside the time. Honor yourself and your beautiful life by etching out a precious block of time.

Nourish

I prepare to create with the Divine.

Want More?

In this precious time of preparation, feed yourself with your favorite sacred texts and mystical poetry. Your heart knows what it wants to hear. Listen to the wisdom of your heart.

Day 30

soul day
and intention mandala

The practice is to touch life deeply so that the Kingdom of God becomes a reality. This is not a matter of devotion. It is a matter of practice. The Kingdom of God is available here and now.

—Thich Nhat Hanh, *Living Buddha, Living Christ*

Awake in Joy

As the light pulls you from sleep, lie still with your eyes closed and allow your dreams and other thoughts to come to you. Stay in that delicious, theta-drenched state until you feel you have received all the information heaven gathered for you in the night.

As you rise, feel the light, experiencing it as Spirit kissing your cheeks and welcoming you to another day on this gorgeous blue globe. Announce out loud that today is a glorious day.

Look at your nighttime notepad. Did you write anything down? Would you like to record anything that came through this morning while you were lying in theta?

Begin with Prayers and Intention

As you step into the space where you are going to plant the seeds of your abundant future, bless it; thank it for supporting you during this sacred time. Honor the space and the time by lighting a candle, ringing a bell, dancing around the room, saying a blessing—something to name the space and the day holy.

Send Soul Slinky waves of intention for a beautiful day filled with wisdom and grace. Even before you begin, feel gratitude for the day ahead and all that will happen. Send waves back and forth between your intention and gratitude hands. Get your angels and guides into the act. Feel them smiling and laughing and playing with the Soul Slinky with you.

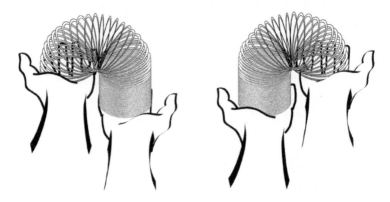

Call the Divine to be with you as you begin the next stage in your soul's grand adventure on earth. My favorite way to do this is to play *The Ghandarva Experience* by Tom Kenyon. With his astonishing voice, Tom calls in saints and divine beings from all traditions. After twelve minutes, the room positively vibrates with presence. I play this CD at the beginning of all my important projects and sacred gatherings, including the writing of this book.

Take your time creating sacred space not just in the room, but also in you. Don't rush. Breathe deeply, pray from the heart, dance, meditate, burn sage, light incense, sing, ring bells, talk aloud to Spirit, call on your guides and angels—do anything that feels right to set the tone for a deep soul experience.

Ask for an Opening Message

Begin your Soul Day with a sacred reading. Perhaps you'd like to spend more time with *You Are Here* or *Blessings of the Cosmos.* Perhaps Hafiz or Rumi or another mystical poet is beckoning you to sit, so he or she can whisper in your ear. Or perhaps you feel led to contemplate the words of a sacred text, or pull an oracle card, or find the meaning of an ancient rune from *The Book of Runes* by Ralph Blum. Ask Spirit to guide you to just what you need to read as you begin your Soul Day. It will be the perfect message for this moment, but it may be a surprise. And you may not know till the day is over just how perfect your opening message was.

Step into Divine Dialogue

When you feel ready, enter the heart of your Soul Day with three long deep-soul-writing conversations with your divine Voice. You've been accessing divine guidance through deep soul writing for several weeks now, so you know how effective it can be. But something extraordinary happens when you have extended conversations. When I read *Science and the Akashic Field,* I began to understand from a quantum standpoint why and how deep soul writing works. Ervin Laszlo explains, "[W]hen the censorship of the waking consciousness is not operative, information can reach the mind from almost any part or aspect of the universe."

Well, when you engage in these three extensive divine dialogues, your conscious censor will have no choice but to get out of the way, and amazing information can and will come through. In the first conversation, you will review what you experienced and learned when you uncovered the gifts of your past and untied knots of unforgiveness. This is a beautiful opportunity to see the past as the Buddha sees it—as the food of your present and your future. In the second conversation, you will talk about what happened when you looked forward. Then, in the richest conversation of all, you will identify how you want to live—the conditions that will nurture your beautiful life.

There is no set list of questions to ask or outline to follow. Even if I gave you one, your soul and Voice would steer the conversation where it needs to go. But here are a few thoughts to get you started. The most important thing is to take the time to have deep dialogue. No matter how excited you are about making your mandala, don't jump ahead. You have created a space where the Divine has your undivided attention for a significant block of time. You are now more open and receptive than you have ever been. Your conscious censor is asleep. This is a rare and precious moment. Stay in it and receive all its gifts.

Each of these conversations will be fairly long. Drink lots of water and take breaks whenever you need them.

First Conversation: The Past

> *You are here for life; and if you are here for life,*
> *life will be here for you.*
>
> —Thich Nhat Hanh, *You Are Here*

Thank your Voice and all your angels and guides for being with you on this very special day.

Invite your GrandSelf, your soul—your highest and holiest self—to be fully present and fully open to divine guidance. Tell your Voice that for the remainder of the day your GrandSelf is in charge and that together your GrandSelf and beloved Voice are going to design a beautiful life filled with purpose and joy.

Begin by reviewing what has brought you to this moment:

- Pull out your original intention for the Lotus and the Lily and talk about how that intention has evolved or changed since you began.

- One last time, look back together, reviewing the gifts of the past. Does the wisdom of the Tao, "Everything is a movement toward your wholeness," mean something more to you now? Say thank you for your story because it brought you to this moment.

- Thank Spirit for helping you release your thought worms.

- Remember all the delightful ways Spirit winked at you. Laugh and say thank you. And pay attention. Your Soul Day will be filled with winks.

This is the perfect time to talk over all you accomplished in the last year. Let your heart be filled with pride for all you have done and learned. It's always a revelation to see just how much happened in twelve months. (If you are repeating this process, it's a fun time to look at last year's name and discover what it really meant.)

Review the gifts of forgiveness. If there's more to discuss about releasing your prisoners, forgiving yourself, or forgiving others, have that conversation. Forgive yourself not only for what you did, but what you didn't get done, too. There's time enough coming to accomplish more than you ever dreamed possible.

Thank Spirit for all your universe cash and ask for guidance to spend it wisely.

Second Conversation: The Future

> O beloved Pan, and all the other deities of this place, grant that I may become beautiful in my soul within, and that all of my external possessions may be in harmony with my inner self.
>
> —Plato

If you know your soul's purpose, say thank you for this precious gift and rededicate yourself to live it. If you don't, this is a lovely time to have a fresh chat about how you bring love and light and joy into the world. Perhaps some new insights into your purpose will come. Or just ask to be of service. That is really all that matters. Perhaps knowing your soul's unique purpose is an item you'd like to put on your mandala. It would be an exciting seed to plant and watch grow over the next year.

Did you play the life-around-the-corner game? Talk over your vision. Bless it. Be grateful for it. Or do the game now. If you don't feel called to have that experience, let it go. This is your Soul Day, and you and your divine guides are in charge.

Look at the cart you filled a few days ago. Pull out each item and review it. Don't be surprised if your desires shift or deepen or change altogether. Here are a few clues that will help you identify something that belongs on your mandala:

- Your heart leaps and your soul tingles in anticipation.
- You smile. If you can't wipe a grin off your face, you're looking at a seed that belongs on your mandala.
- It serves and expresses your soul's purpose or helps you discover what that may be.
- It has potential. It is a seed you'd love to plant and watch grow. Imagining what it could look like in full bloom is exciting.
- Taken together, everything you will put on your mandala moves you closer to your life around the corner.

Don't feel that you have to identify or describe all the good you want in your life. You can't. There is a divine element of surrender at play here. You are not the only creator. If you were, only what you ask for could come to you. But as you will soon discover, if you haven't already, when you focus on creating fertile conditions instead of constantly carrying the burden of asking, all kinds of divine manifestations come to you, whether you ask for them or not. So enjoy this exercise in selecting beautiful desires, but don't worry that you might leave something out. Heaven knows.

Do you have a name for your year? Or is a new name emerging? What name captures the essence of the beautiful life you are creating? What words describe how the landscape will look when all your seeds are planted and they begin to grow and prosper? The name may come now or when you make your mandala.

Third Conversation: Your Conditions

> *When conditions are sufficient there is a manifestation.*
>
> —The Buddha

You are now entering the richest conversation of your Soul Day, the richest conversation of the Lotus and the Lily, and possibly the richest conversation of your entire year. The first time I talked about conditions, I sensed I was having one of the most important conversations of my life. And it was. Knowing my conditions has altered the way I live and set me on a new path, a path I adore and never want to leave.

This is a good time to revisit Jesus's comprehensive teaching on how to live. In *Blessings of the Cosmos*, Neil Douglas-Klotz unravels the phrase "Seek ye first the kingdom of God and his righteousness, and all else shall be added unto you" (Matthew 6:33) down to its core Aramaic words, roots, and concepts. Thanks to his brilliant research, we are able to sit on a hill beside Jesus's first-century listeners and hear what they heard. This is what Douglas-Klotz believes they heard:

If you're going to be anxious and rush around about anything,
do it first about finding the "I can" of the universe
and how it straightens out your life.

Line up your starting place with that of the cosmos:
search and ask and boil with impatience
until you find the vision of the One Being
that empowers all your ideas and ideals,
that restores your faith and justifies your love.

All the rest—the universal and endless "things"
    of life—
will then attach themselves to you as you
    need them.

You will stand at the threshold where
completeness arrives naturally
and prostration leads to perfection.
Pouring yourself out makes the universe do
    the same.

There's a lot more here than "Seek first the kingdom," isn't there? Sit with this translation. Say it aloud. Slowly. Several times. Allow the ideas to settle onto your skin. I've read this hundreds of times, and each time I find it fresh, provocative, and thrilling. On any given day, a different phrase or image will grab me.

Reading "line up your starting place" one day, I realized I wanted to stand directly in front of my mandala and literally line up my heart with the little red heart at the center, which represents Spirit. And when I say the part about endless things attaching themselves, I see those things and feel them flying through the sky and into my life. This phrase matches so elegantly the angels' advice to see only what's coming in. And I love the picture of me standing at the threshold, where it's all natural, all complete, all effortless. I see my toes on that threshold, and my eyes look out in wonder at a perfect, complete world. But my favorite line, the one that takes my breath away every time, is "pouring myself out makes the universe do the same." That image gets me back to my center, my truth, my purpose. It reminds me that when I stop fretting and just pour my small self into the life I'm here to live, the universe lovingly pours its big Self right back onto me. And indeed, this is exactly how my life has worked since I started following the masters' instructions to create my fertile conditions.

In *Blessings of the Cosmos*, Douglas-Klotz pries open key Aramaic words like *malkutah*, translated as "kingdom" in English. Jesus's most startling teaching was the kingdom of God is within. He said this over and over and over—and we're still trying to understand it. In his first book of Aramaic translations, *Prayers of the Cosmos*, Douglas-Klotz dissects the Aramaic phrase *Teytey malkutah*, translated as "Thy kingdom come" in the Lord's Prayer. He explains, "Malkutah refers to . . . ruling principles that guide our lives toward unity. It is what says 'I can' within us and is willing, despite all odds, to take a step in a new direction." Reading Douglas-Klotz's books, I sensed that understanding this concept of kingdom is the key that unlocks the mystery of life. So I asked the masters and teachers of the Akashic Record. Here, verbatim, is what they said:

> The kingdom is the reality of living in the human body but through the everyday laws of Spirit. When one lives following only laws that are human, there is pain, frustration, and agony. When one lives through spiritual laws and divine nature, then the human experience becomes heaven on earth. That is the kingdom. It is bringing that which exists beyond the physical realm with the guidance of Christ-consciousness into the human being.

And what is Christ-consciousness? It is the state of union with the Divine while still in a human body. The Greek word *khristos* means "anointed one." All traditions refer to the Christed state. Hafiz, who was a Sufi Muslim, said, "I am / A hole in a flute / That the Christ's breath moves through" ("A Hole in a Flute," *The Gift*, translation by Daniel Ladinsky).

So your conditions are ways of being that move you toward an awareness of unity. They are how you pour yourself out. They are the actions you take every day to find the "I can" of the universe and align yourself to it. They are the ways you bring divine Light into your everyday life. They are the ways you create heaven on earth.

My conditions sound like actions; they are things I do every day:

I live in intention.

I say my prayers out loud.

I work in sacred space.

I do my holy work.

I focus only on what's coming in.

I have a grateful heart.

But your conditions don't have to be actions or activities. Just as most people's soul purpose is a way of being, not a job, most people's conditions are ways they approach life, filters through which they see and experience the Divine within the human experience. For example, Jazz Jaeschke in Austin, Texas, has four conditions:

Observe

Accept

Trust

Create

Jazz made collage images that remind her visually of how to live her four conditions. On a separate piece of paper, she wrote a full, rich explanation. When she works with her

mandala, she speaks her conditions aloud. You can hear in
her descriptions how living these conditions creates heaven
on earth for her. Here is Jazz Jaeschke's delightful mandala,
"Harmony Happens."

"Harmony Happens"
Jazz Jaeschke, Austin, Texas

The four squares in the center circle are her conditions.
From the upper left clockwise, they are:

Observe: I am one who commits to Spirit to pay close
attention to the little details as well as the overall forest, to
be receptive to nature as well as technology for clues to the
puzzles of daily life and for guidance in the larger, more
significant mysteries of being in human form.

Accept: I am one who commits to Spirit to accept what comes my way as what's best for me overall, including dreary matters that dampen my mood. I am one who knows that metamorphosis takes time and the caterpillar cannot understand that it will become a butterfly. I am one who waits out storms, knowing an angel will eventually arrive and bring transformation to place into my lap.

Create: I am one who commits to Spirit my heart and talents to the best of my abilities to convey Spirit's messages through poetry, prose, collage, fabric constructions, solutions to mechanical and emotional dilemmas, and any other creative way that can serve to channel Spirit through me to others.

Trust: I am one who commits to Spirit to trust that whatever is happening is what's supposed to be happening, even when it seems otherwise at the moment, and to trust that I will know what I need to know and that I do not need to know all the answers to what has happened and what will happen. I am one who needs only to trust Spirit to catch me when I leap.

Here are some ideas that may help you have a rich dialogue about your conditions. Choose any that speak to you or just pick up a pen, ask a question, and allow the conversation to unfold.

Begin by talking over your understanding of the concept of conditions. Don't swallow my definition or my enthusiasm. Explore this idea on the page until you feel comfortable with what conditions mean for you and the impact they will have on your life. Until and unless you feel they are important, they won't and can't influence your life.

Then talk about your individual conditions. This is a deeply personal conversation. No one can tell you what your conditions are. Only your soul knows the fertile environment it wants—*needs*—to create an abundant life. You can look at other people's conditions to get some ideas for how they phrase them, but don't copy anyone else's conditions. Their conditions create and nourish *their* life. You are creating and nourishing *your* life, and there is no other life quite like yours. There is no other soul like yours. No one else has your purpose, your gifts, your dreams, your vision. No one else can do what you are here to do.

After all the rich soul exploration you've done in the last few weeks, your conditions may tumble quickly onto the page. If not, perhaps these questions will help you discover your fertile conditions.

- What is truly important to me? How do I want to live?

- How can I stay aligned with Spirit? How can I line myself up with the starting point? How do I want to live every day to be in a vibrant state of divine partnership?

- How can I create the life I want? How can I keep my soul fields nourished? What do I need to do, or be, to become fertile and ready to grow into my full potential?

- What can I do every day to be of real service?

- How am I living when I feel most fully alive?

- What do I feel called to do every day? What are my guides and angels encouraging me to do?

- How does my soul want to create a beautiful, abundant life?

Your conditions will probably start out as fairly long descriptive paragraphs, but eventually they'll distill down to a sentence or a phrase—maybe even a word. For example, my conditions are abbreviated on my mandala as *Intention, Prayer, Sacred Space, Holy Work, Focus, Grateful Heart.*

You don't need a lot of conditions. In the end, there are probably four to eight states or actions you want to renew every day to live a life aligned with the "I can" of the universe. If you go beyond eight, you'll end up with more than you can consciously live every day. And if you don't live them every day, you won't create the fertile soil in which your seeds can grow. If you sense you have too many, ask your Voice to help you edit.

You'll know when you've identified your conditions. Your heart will soar with joy, knowing *this* is how you want to live. *This* is how you "pursue a right relationship with the Universal One." *This* is the life that cannot help but magnetically attract all the support and love the universe has in store for you. You'll feel your angels and guides clapping and nodding in joyful agreement. Don't second-guess yourself. If your conditions feel right, they are right.

Find a Symbol for Your Conditions

Once you've identified your conditions, talk over the ideal image for them. This image will be the center of your mandala. For me, it is a lily. I have six conditions, and my favorite mystical symbol, the lily, has six petals. I fell in love with the lily in my first angel reading in November, 2008, a few months before *Writing Down Your Soul* came out. I was in a financial pickle and kept asking questions about money. No matter what I asked, Michael answered in a booming voice, "You don't understand how important this book is!" Finally, in total frustration, I screamed back, "Okay! I don't understand how important this book is! I don't! But how am I supposed to live?!"

I am ashamed to admit I argued with an archangel. But I'm glad I did because what he said next was so precious. He lowered his voice and gently said, "You are a lily." He didn't have to say another word. I know the story. When people were complaining about their struggles to get food and clothes, Jesus said, "Consider the lilies. They do not toil nor spin, yet I tell you Solomon in all his glory was not arrayed as one of them. So think, if this is what your father will do for the flowers which are today in the field and tomorrow in the fire, think what your father will do for you" (Luke 12:27). Since that day, I've kept lilies on my altar.

The lily is a universal spiritual symbol. In Christian art, Archangel Gabriel is depicted presenting a lily to Mary at the Annunciation. The lily represents fertility in the tarot and is a symbol of motherhood in Greek mythology. It is often seen as a symbol of trinity because it has two sets of three petals. I asked the masters and teachers of the Akashic Record about the lily. They said the lily is our "divine antenna, reaching up to the Light." They said we all have a lily floating over our heads. Indeed, many Eastern depictions of the chakras show a lotus or water lily floating over the head. The masters and teachers said the lily has "very, very, very high vibration," but they also said each person gets to select her own perfect image for her conditions.

What is the perfect symbol of your conditions? For many, it simply jumps up and announces itself. Sometimes it's an image the person has always loved, like a star, a dove, or a heart. Thanks to the Buddha and Jesus, the lotus and the lily have sprouted in the center of many mandalas. But for most people, the image is a surprise. It was for Sophia Bailey of Christchurch, New Zealand. One frond of a koru, a silver fern native to New Zealand, insisted on being at the center of her mandala. She thought that was strange until she looked it up. The koru symbolizes new life, growth, strength, and peace—all attributes Sophia wants in her life. But there was something more. In an email she wrote, "The circular shape of the koru frond conveys the idea of perpetual movement to me, but the inner coil reminds me to return always to the point of origin."

Ask your guides and angels to show you the perfect image. Then look around. Talk it over with your Voice and see what happens. Together you will stumble upon the perfect image for your promise to live in a way that nurtures your beautiful, meaningful, abundant life. If the image doesn't want to come, take a break, go for a walk, or take a nap and ask as you fall asleep. Your guides will lead you to the image. And it may be a surprise.

Make Your Intention Mandala

Hafiz,
Look at the Perfect One
At the Circle's Center:

He Spins and Whirls like a Golden Compass,
Beyond all that is Rational,

To show this dear world

That Everything,
Everything in Existence
Does point to God.

—Hafiz, from "A Golden Compass," *I Heard God Laughing,*
Translation by Daniel Ladinsky

You are now ready to design and construct an Intention Mandala that is infused with everything you long to bring to life. This is fun—divine fun. I rather imagine the Buddha and Jesus are laughing, and I'm confident Jung and Hafiz approve, too.

Start by considering where you're going to put your mandala. Ideally, you want room to stand in front of it as you say your daily prayers, and it's lovely to have it in your sight throughout your day. My 2006 mandala was a piece of 8 1/2 x 11 paper taped to my bedroom wall. It worked wonders, but when I sat down to create my 2010 mandala, I wanted something bigger and more visually compelling. And I wanted it on the wall next to my computer so it could feed me all day. So I got a pad of 11 x 17 paper. I've made three mandalas from that pad, but for 2012, I want to make one that spins. That requires firmer paper, so I'm cutting circles out of colored poster board and pinning them at the center to a thin piece of foam board a little bigger than the circles. When I'm finished, I'll attach the whole thing to the wall next to my computer. People have made mandalas from twelve inches in diameter to three feet. Others have made them out of different materials altogether. Alice Manning in San Francisco made hers out of clay. Really!

Here are my simple directions on how to make a mandala. You, however, might be more creative and artistic. Perhaps you want to make a globe or a mobile hanging from the ceiling. Perhaps like Jazz you can work with computer graphics. Don't feel constricted in any way by my ultra-simple cut, draw, color, pin method. Follow your intuition.

But don't get lost in this as a craft project that never gets done. There's something powerful and exciting about having all these rich conversations, getting clarity about your conditions and desires, and capturing all of it on a mandala in one compressed period of time. You know what happens when you say, "I'll get to it." You don't. Within a day or two, you want to be praying with your mandala, setting it in motion, living your conditions, watering your seeds, and watching it all come to life, not wondering when you'll find time to complete it. So enjoy every minute making your mandala but remember: this is an easy, fun soul projection, not a complicated art project.

Here's my method.

Step 1: Cut the Circles and Backing

If you're making a mandala that spins, cut the foam board and the circles that will fit inside it. The foam board can be any shape—rectangular, round, hexagon. Have fun with the shape of the backing, but the mandala itself should be a circle.

To make the circles for the mandala—a larger, outer one for desires and a smaller, inner one for conditions—use a compass or trace a dinner plate and soup bowl. The core element is the inner circle of conditions, so make sure it's big enough to hold the symbol of your conditions. If you're not sure, do a couple practice sketches. Or go online and find an image to cut out. I know, I said to keep the computer off, but last year my handmade attempts at a lotus were pretty bad, so I found a huge purple lotus and an even bigger magenta one online, printed them in color, cut them out, and pasted my handmade lily on top. I love the way the edges of all three curl up as if they are reaching out to me.

I write my six conditions on the six petals of my yellow lily, but not everyone writes his conditions *on* his symbol. There was no room to write on Sophia Bailey's koru frond, so she wrote her conditions in phrases that radiate out from the frond like sunbeams.

Leave a little room on the side of your mandala for embellishments or decorations. One year, I wanted to add wings around the circle like angels were protecting me, but it was a tight squeeze because I'd only left an inch border. Give yourself room. You never know what divine ideas might pour into you at the last minute.

Step 2: Put Your Desires on the Outer Circle

Write words and/or images of what you want on the outer rim of the larger circle. I typically have twelve so it's easy to mark off where the twelve positions would be if my circle were a clock. Here's an image of the outer circle with spots for eight desires.

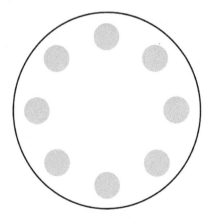

the lotus and the lily

Lots of people cut out pictures from magazines. I know my little stick figures are terribly plain, but I have trouble finding commercial images that match the ones in my head. Plus, I want the images to come out of my hand just like my divine dialogue does, so I draw little two-inch figures or images and add a few words to describe them.

My drawings are simple—but powerful. For example, on my 2010 "Breakthrough Year" mandala I wrote "Perfect Agent" and drew two hands clasping. That conveyed the essence of the warm, partnership relationship I wanted, but left everything else to Spirit. Three months later, Spirit delivered Nancy Barton, and, oh, is she ever the perfect literary agent! I wrote "Radiant Health" and drew a one-inch green figure with golden lines radiating all around her. By the end of the year, with no diet or exercise regimen, my body had returned to the weight and shape I had in my thirties.

On my 2011 "Big Pot" mandala I drew a little yellow, curving road with a tiny stick figure, representing my son walking on it, and labeled it "Jerry is Safe, Free, and Loved." He called on Thanksgiving Day. Before I could say hello, he blurted out, "Don't worry, Mom, I'm safe!" His apartment was destroyed in a fire, but he and his possessions were safe. You can be sure I'm keeping my son on that yellow road under the word *Safe* on all future mandalas.

I color my drawings with a big set of colored pencils I've had for years. This is as crafty as I get, but you might want to get a bit more elaborate. Beth Reilly used crayons, colored pencils, and magic markers, but her finished design is elegant and evocative. On Beth's mandala, everything leads in to and out from a gorgeous path in the woods, which represents her journey to Source. Her conditions are Love, Intimate Connection, Blessing, and Gratitude. Her twelve seeds of desire are (from the twelve o'clock position): Live Deeply, Love, Prosperity, Home, Health, Travel, Creativity, School, Work, Self-discovery, Spirituality, and Relationships.

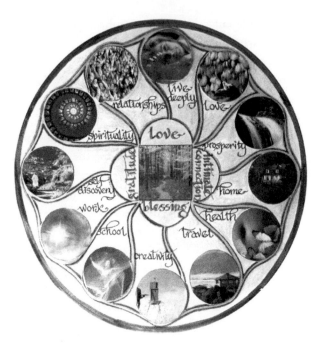

"A Year of Living Deeply"
Beth Reilly, Bradenton, Florida

When I asked Beth how she made her mandala, she said,

I tried to let deep feelings lead me. I did a lot of soul
writing about my values and desires. Then I ripped photos out of magazines that appealed to me—anything and
everything, and lots of them. I whittled the pile down
to twelve photos that resonated. I tried not to let my
analytical brain have too much control; I just let it figure out placement and symmetry. I let what each photo
would represent be totally guided by the inner Voice;
thus, I ended up with surprises, like the joyous dancer
in "School" and an abdomen in "Health." The colors
I used in the mandala were also what felt right—pink
for conditions sending pink rivers out to my whole life,
light teal in the segments, all wrapped in a dark blue
border. It was so much fun and ultimately so power-

the lotus and the lily

ful. I devoted a good bit of time to it that day, but it was well worth it.

Step 3: Put Your Conditions on the Inner Circle

Draw or paste the image or images of your conditions on the inner circle. If you're not certain how it's going to look, make a few samples. It took me several attempts to make my lily petals fat enough to hold my six words. And I added several small circles at the base of the flower to symbolize the unifying force of the universe. Last, I drew a tiny red heart at the very center of the lily and of the whole mandala. That little red heart reminds me that I come from divine love and to divine love I will return.

Illustrate your conditions in any way you feel led. The only thing that matters is that the image speaks to you, lifts your heart, and inspires you to want to bring those conditions to life. So choose any shapes, images, or colors that call to you.

Here's a simple outline of a six-figured Flower of Life to give you an idea of the smaller circle for your conditions.

When Catherine Anderson of Charlotte, North Carolina, began to identify her conditions, they grew until they took over her mandala. She began by cutting a large orange poster board circle, because she wanted to work on her second chakra that year. She added eight circular images, each describing how she wanted to live. For example, she pasted a scene of water gently flowing around rocks and added the words "Living in Flow." She pasted a photo of a spider web and the words "Creating a

Community of Divine Connectivity." My favorite is a picture of Tibetan prayer flags flapping in the wind with "Trusting My Prayers to the Wind." At the center, she put a dark orange circle with telescoping circles that draw the eye into a bright light at the center. She pasted a small Buddha sitting on a lotus in that light. She named her year "My Year of Connecting to Mystical Wisdom." In Catherine's mandala, her conditions are her desires and her desires are her conditions, and they are all circles. If one circle has power, Catherine's mandala has uber-power, and indeed, Catherine reported that the year brought mystical opportunities she could never have predicted when she made this mandala.

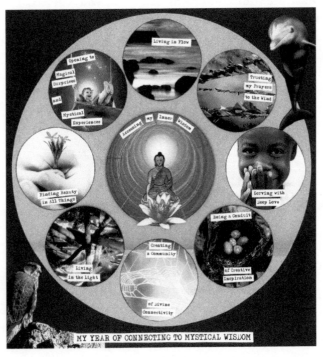

"My Year of Connecting to Mystical Wisdom"
Catherine Anderson, Charlotte, North Carolina

Step 4: Add the Name of Your Year

Do you have a name for your year? Has a new name poked its head into the process as you've been making your mandala? If you're not sure, sit back and look at your mandala as a whole. Imagine what your life will look like and feel like as you live your conditions and your desires begin to organically grow. Visualize your mandala coming to life. What phrase or sentence captures that life? Don't question the thought that comes. It's almost always a surprise.

Here's a simple image of how you might place the components of your mandala on a foam backing.

NAME OF YEAR

Step 5: Decorate Your Mandala

Stand back and look at your mandala. Is there anything you'd like to add? Any colors, shapes, images? Would you like to add a symbol of your angels or guides? Catherine Anderson thought her mandala was complete, but suddenly she felt a dolphin and hawk calling to her. She cut out pictures of both and pasted the dolphin on the top right corner and the hawk on the bottom left. When they landed on her mandala, she felt it was complete.

If you're not sure how your extras will look, draw them on other paper and cut and paste. Or you might decide you like it spare. It's your mandala—create it any way you want.

Plant Your Seeds

When your mandala is finished, stop and look at it. Just look at it. Allow it to speak to you, feed you, excite you, inspire you. Let its energy wash over you for a moment. It's beautiful, isn't it? But as beautiful as it is, it isn't yet fully alive. It needs one last piece of intention embedded in it. It is waiting for you to purposefully plant your seeds. Do this by slowly, prayerfully, speaking each desire aloud and calling on your divine partner, angels, and guides to be your witnesses as you call each desire into life. Then press down with your hand, pushing your desire into the mandala as if you were pushing a seed into the earth. Tap the paper as you would tap a seed freshly planted in soil. This is the moment your mandala comes alive. This is the moment it begins to grow.

Hafiz has the perfect prayer for planting your seeds. I discovered it when I completed my "Big Pot" mandala and asked Hafiz for a final blessing. I burst out laughing when I opened *The Gift* to these lines:

It used to be
That when I would wake in the morning
I could with confidence say,
"What am 'I' going to
Do?

That was before the seed
Cracked open.

Now Hafiz is certain

There are two of us housed
In this body,

Doing the shopping together in the market and
Tickling each other
While fixing the evening's food.

Now when I awake
All the internal instruments play the same music:

"God, what love-mischief can 'We' do
For the world
Today?"

—Hafiz, "The Seed Cracked Open," *The Gift*,
Translation by Daniel Ladinsky

I printed this poem on bright orange paper, drew a tiny brown seed with a green sprout and roots coming out of it, and pasted the sheet to the top of my mandala. When I walk in my office in the morning, I say, "Okay, Spirit, what are *we* going to do today!"

Write Your Mandala Prayer

Your mandala is much more than a symbol or picture. It is a three-dimensional, spinning sphere. It is alive with all that your soul loves and longs to create. It is alive with your personal vision of the One Being that empowers all your ideals and justifies your love. It is alive with your commitment to yourself to live a life of fertile conditions that nourish all your seeds. It is your very own engine of change. It will feed you every day. Just by being in your presence, it will send you subconscious messages, reminders, and encouragement. But to experience its full power and potential, you want to have a conscious relationship with it as well.

I talk to my mandala every day. It is an integral part of my morning practice. I do this because I take to heart the Buddha's instructions to pray with 100 percent of my being, so that my speech becomes a mantra with the power to transform reality. You have created a mandala that has the power to transform reality. Just think how powerful it can be when you add a mantra with the power to transform reality!

Here's what I do. I stand in front of my mandala, line my heart up with the center, and speak my opening declaration:

> I am one.
>
> You are One.
>
> We are one.
>
> I am one with the One.
>
> Together we create a beautiful world.

Then I talk over the things I want for a moment or two. But after a while, I hand them over to Spirit saying, "Listen, I know you are taking care of all this and more. What I want is not my job. My job today is to live my conditions." And I sing this little chant:

(I touch my first fingers together.)—Aum, I live in intention.

(My second fingers.)—Aum, I say my prayers out loud.

(Ring fingers.)—Aum, I work in sacred space.

(Little fingers.)—Aum, I do my holy work.

(Thumbs.)—And I see only, only, only what's coming in.

(At this point, my hands are pressed together in prayer position and I bring my
   hands to my heart as I finish my song.)—And I have a grateful heart.

My chant is simple and deeply personal. (On my website, you can see a video of me chanting it.) When I pray this way, every speck of me is in my prayer. My body is in motion, my hands create a mudra, my voice lifts to the heavens, my heart bursts with joy, my mind is totally focused, and my imagination takes me into the center of my mandala, where I see my whole new world. I'm certain Lord Buddha would approve.

He must love Laura Harvey's mandala prayer practice. Laura gets up before her family, goes in her meditation room, and turns on lively music. Then for three or four minutes, Laura and God dance. With music playing in the background, she then renews her conditions. This is Laura's mandala prayer:

Because conditions must be present for manifestation to occur,
I make the following covenant to my Spirit.
Every day I will:
Shake off my ego and free my Spirit.
   I dance!
Boldly speak my Truth to myself and the Universe.
   I pray out loud.
Bring to mind the divine assistance, support and resources available to me.
   I am not alone. I ask for help. .
Have clear intentions and head in the direction of my dreams.
   I take action toward my goals.
Be aware of the present moment, grounded and mindful.
   I enter into the Silence.
See the good and celebrate wholeness.
   I am grateful.

This is Catherine Anderson's prayer for "My Year of Connecting to Mystical Wisdom." Notice how it weaves together all her conditions:

Serving with deep love, I access my inner wisdom easily through my daily meditative and creative practices. I invite magical surprises and mystical experiences into my life. As a conduit of creative inspiration, I surround myself with a web of divine connections that flow to me at the perfect time and place. Beauty and light surround me, and my prayers are always heard. And So It Is.

How will you live with your mandala? If a prayer or blessing or song or dance makes itself known, capture it. In the next few days, as you build your relationship with your mandala, you will finalize your practice. For now, just be open to the possibilities. And if the day is ending and you don't have time, let this go for now. In the next chapter, you will create your daily spiritual practice that sends your mandala out into the universe where it can—and will—transform your life.

Bless Your Mandala

At the end of his explanation of "Seek first the kingdom" in *Blessings of the Cosmos*, Neil Douglas-Klotz offers this summary:

> Here Jesus says that when we pursue a right relationship with the Universal One and allow this relationship to realign our lives, we produce a condition of receptivity in which anything we need to help us complete our purpose in life will be supplied by the universe.

The first time I read this summary, it felt like a blessing. I have read this paragraph to myself probably more than any other single quotation. On mornings when I need help finding my center, I stand in front of my mandala and speak this blessing aloud. It always lifts and inspires me. When people share their mandalas in my classes, I ask them if they'd like a blessing from Yeshua. (*Yeshua* is *Jesus* in Aramaic.) I alter the words as if Yeshua were speaking directly to the person. For example, when Beth Reilly shared her mandala, I said,

> Beth,
> When you pursue a right relationship with the Universal One and allow this relationship to realign your life, you produce a condition of receptivity, and everything you need to fulfill your purpose in life will be supplied by the universe.

It always feels like Yeshua is right there blessing each person and each mandala. It's a very holy moment. You can do this blessing for yourself. If these words speak to you, say them aloud, as if Jesus or the Buddha or any other spiritual master were right there in front of you, looking you in the eye and showering you with love.

This is not the only way to receive a blessing for your mandala. You can ask for a blessing and randomly open a sacred text or mystical poetry anthology. You can ask your angels and guides to bless your mandala in an oracle card reading. Or ask the Voice for a blessing on the page.

Post Your Mandala

When your mandala is complete and blessed, place it where you'll see it and work with it every day. Create a little ceremony to honor its arrival in your home and in your life. Perhaps you'd like to perform the preparation ritual you created back in Week 1. That would be a delightful way to bring all your Lotus and the Lily experiences full circle.

If you'd like to see your mandala in other locations, make color copies, print out a photo, or make mini-versions. I've pinned a copy to my bedroom wall so it feeds me while I sleep.

Celebrate

Conclude your Soul Day in gratitude and joy. Send those Soul Slinky waves of gratitude flying! You have been heard, supported, and guided to stand in deep spiritual truth, declare the life you want, and commit to the conditions that will nourish all you want and more. It's been a big and holy day. Celebrate.

Begin with a little dance. Yes, dance. Dance is the ultimate expression of joy. Remember Snoopy? He danced when he was happy. Are you feeling happy? So dance! It might be just a little skip down the hall or a twirl in private where no one can see. Doesn't matter. Just dance.

Then eat in joy. Have a delightful meal and toast the blessings of the abundant life coming to you. I always make a feast to conclude my Soul Day. I put on my favorite music and laugh and sing as I chop and sizzle. And I treat myself with a good bottle of wine. I set the table with my mother's Waterford crystal, and I celebrate not only the day, but also the whole glorious year to come. And I invite all my angels and guides to come to the table and celebrate with me. I leave two chairs empty next to me, like the place at a Seder meal that is reserved for Elijah, and I invite Archangels Michael and Gabriel to sit. And if it's twilight, I know my cardinal parents will come and sing their delight. If my son is visiting, he has an honored place at the table. My whole family, spiritual and physical, present and passed, is invited to my Soul Day party.

Finally, sleep. Sleep the sleep of the blessed. As you drift off, breathe prayers of gratitude for your Soul Day experience and ask for any last messages in your dreams.

Tomorrow, you will begin the grand adventure of living with your Intention Mandala and watching all the seeds you've planted grow. Miracles are on their way.

Nourish

I create with the Divine.

Want More?

It has been a full and perfect day. But if, as you are drifting off, you find you want one more gift, reread the blessing you requested at the beginning of your Soul Day. Perhaps now it will make perfect sense.

how to keep your intention mandala alive

The key to transforming your life isn't going through the four weeks of soul play you've done, rich as they have been. Nor is it creating an Intention Mandala, beautiful as it may be. The key is bringing all you've learned and all you've created to life. This is what your soul wants. It wants to create life. It wants to create a life of heaven on earth.

The masters and teachers of the Akashic Record described heaven on earth as living a fully human life following spiritual, not human, laws. Well, this entire adventure has been a deep swim in profound spiritual laws as lived and taught by great masters. You have learned much. But if you stopped now, set your mandala aside, and didn't revisit it, I don't think much would happen, at least not over the long term. And my intention in sharing this process with you is to help you create a whole, abundant, soul-directed life—not just for today, but for all your days. This is the landscape that lies beyond the Law of Attraction. This is the fertile field of the soul.

So the real soul play begins now. When St. Teresa of Avila said, "The realized soul can play with this universe like a child can a ball," it must have rattled everyone around her. It's still a radical concept. But in light of our understanding of our holographic universe, it makes perfect sense.

Throughout the Lotus and the Lily, you have converted the wisdom of masters and mystics into spiritual practices that speak to your soul. Now you get to create the most powerful practice of all—your own deeply personal, multisensory, daily mandala prayer practice. This is the practice that will nourish and renew your conditions and bring all the seeds you've planted to life. Our guide for how to do this is the Buddha, who taught us to pray with 100 percent of our beings so that our prayers become mantra, a sacred formula with the power to transform reality. We know that the mandala is a visual engine of change with the power to transform reality. Now we are adding full-body prayer that also has the power to transform reality. We're giving ourselves a double dose of transformation.

The key here is that you engage every bit of you—body, breath, emotions, voice, everything you've got. This is fun, and when prayer is fun, we are more inclined to do it. But there is a deeper reason. In his book of Celtic wisdom, *Anam Cara*, John O'Donohue, notes, "The soul is not simply within the body, hidden somewhere within its recesses. The truth is rather the converse. Your body is in the soul, and the soul suffuses you completely. Therefore, all around you there is a secret and beautiful soul-light."

Your soul and your body are united fully in this human experience, so when you step before your mandala, engage your whole embodied soul-light self in your prayers. How do you do that? Well, here are a few ideas. Take any of them that speak to you and add your own. Create something that makes your whole soul-light sing with joy.

Breath

[F]ormally the word [Yahweh] was not spoke at all, but breathed! *Many are convinced that its correct pronunciation is an attempt to replicate and imitate the very sound of inhalation and exhalation. The one thing we do every moment of our lives is therefore to speak the name of God.*

—Richard Rohr, *The Naked Now*

Everything begins with the breath. With every breath, you announce, "I am here. I am an embodied soul reveling in this human experience." So begin at the beginning and take a few sweet breaths as you step in front of your mandala. Plus, as Andrew Newberg tells us in *How God Changes Your Brain*, slow, deep breathing replenishes neural energy and reduces stress. Take a breath, and instantly you will feel more centered and ready to connect.

Words

A world lives within you. No one else can bring you news of this inner world. Through the opening of the mouth, we bring out sounds from the mountain beneath the soul. These sounds are words.

—John O'Donohue, *Anam Cara*

If you wrote a mandala prayer on your Soul Day, revisit it. Or write one now. But don't leave words out of your mandala practice. Your visuals and your words are two equal parts of a creative whole.

My words of my prayers come in three sections. First, I make my declaration of being one with the One, then I talk over my desires and hand them to Spirit, and last I sing my conditions in a little chant. My declaration is on a little card, but the rest are not written. The conversation with Spirit in front of my mandala is an extemporaneous chat that changes every day based on what's happening, and my conditions song is so short and musical that I can't forget it. But most people have a written prayer that they refer to until it becomes a part of their being. My only suggestion is keep it short. There's big power in a short prayer.

Voice

So it is with the word that goes from my mouth: it will not return to me unfulfilled or before having carried out my good pleasure and having achieved what it was sent to do.

—Isaiah 55:11

Whatever words you use, don't think them, *speak* them. There's a time in your spiritual life for silent meditation; this is not it. Speak your words aloud. Speak them with oomph and meaning and heart because spoken words have real generative power. The ancient Hebrews knew this. They described creation exquisitely as an immediate response to God's spoken word. A few millennia later, Yogananda, the yogi who helped bring the wisdom of the East to the West, wrote at length about the generative quality of the human voice in *Autobiography of a Yogi:*

> The infinite potencies of sound derive from the Creative Word, *Aum*, the cosmic vibratory power behind all atomic energies. Any word spoken with clear realization and deep concentration has a materializing value. . . . The *Aum* vibration that reverberates throughout the universe has three manifestations or *gunas*, those of creation, preservation, and destruction. Each time a man utters a word he puts into operation one of the three qualities of *Aum*. This is the lawful reason behind the injunction of all scriptures that man should speak the truth. (Original italics)

John O'Donohue says the same thing, but in a sweet Celtic way. "Each person brings sound out of silence and coaxes the invisible to become visible," he says in *Anam Cara*. You are coaxing the invisible to become visible, so use your voice.

If you've been a silent pray-er, just speaking your prayers aloud can be an adventure. But if you want to go all the way, sing them. In all the ancient monastic traditions, monks sang gorgeous rhythmic chants. If you'd like to hear truly sacred music, listen to Gregorian or Byzantine chants, ancient Sanskrit chants sung by Deva Premal, or the transcendental melodies written by Hildegard of Bingen in the twelfth century. As you listen, notice how sweet the music is and how easy to follow. Once the pattern gets inside you, it wants to ride out on your breath. Let it.

Spiritual singing is powerful medicine. Andrew Newberg discovered why: singing and spiritual practice stimulate the anterior cingulate, the most evolved part of the human brain. An active anterior cingulate tamps down the fear that pours constantly out of our ancient fight-or-flight limbic brain. "It is essential that you nurture that inner negotiator, which is what meditation and spiritual practices do," he writes in *How God Changes Your Brain*. "They strengthen the frontal lobe—which stimulates the anterior cingulate—and this allows you to pursue your conscious goals in life with greater purpose and serenity. A strong frontal-anterior cingulate circuit also inhibits anxiety, depression, and rage."

Emotion

> Soul enters life from below, through the cracks, finding an opening into life at the points where smooth functioning breaks down.
>
> —Thomas Moore, *Care of the Soul*

As I step in front of my mandala, I feel joy. I can't help it. It's so beautiful and so precious to me. As I spin it, I imagine my sphere taking off into space attracting all that resonates with it. Even before I've said a word, I'm smiling. Then, as I talk about my desires and thank Spirit for how they are growing, I feel delight. If I'm concerned about something, I feel the concern, but then I hand the problem to Spirit knowing it is being taken care of. I feel hope, relief, care. I feel *loved*.

Including your emotions may sound obvious, but don't gloss over this. It's an important and often controversial point. Many spiritual leaders encourage us to express only positive emotions because expressing negative ones will just increase them. The problem with this approach is that our negative emotions don't go away just because we pretend we don't feel them. Not only do they not go away, but they also fester in their underground vaults. Your best opportunity to transmute them is in this kind of total prayer. Show up as you are, feeling what you're feeling. Don't cover up your suffering. If you're feeling anger or pain, bring your anger or pain. But share it with the Divine and ask how to heal it.

I once experienced a vicious bout of jealousy. I ran to my mandala and screamed, "I will *not* live like this. Take this away!" The phone rang the next morning. I heard a story that was exactly what I needed to hear. And the jealousy dissolved instantly. Fear won't have dominion for long in this kind of prayer practice. Show up as you are. Show up as all of you. Pray naked. You'll be astonished at the transformation that happens when you do.

Body

> *Your body is the home of your soul on earth.*
> —John O'Donohue, *Anam Cara*

I stand when I pray. I stand in front of my altar. I stand in front of my mandala. I stand when I open the blinds and say my first prayer of the morning. I didn't consciously set out to pray this way; I just like the way I feel praying on my feet. When I stand, it feels like I'm coming to an altar, looking Spirit in the eye, and declaring, "I'm here!" It feels like I am truly connecting to something holy. And I find I can't stand still. Somehow, without directing it, my body starts swaying to the rhythm of the words I speak or the song I sing. My arms start lifting, and sometimes I even start dancing. To move in this open, full surrender to the meaning and power of the words, I need privacy. You've heard the saying, "Dance like nobody's watching." Well, I say, pray like nobody's watching. But you might want to close the door.

Of course, you don't have to stand. Perhaps you're in a wheelchair or don't feel steady on your feet. Perhaps you'd rather fall to your knees or slip into the yogic child's pose or bend to the East. It doesn't matter. Listen to your body and follow what it directs you to do. The point is to bring your whole self into your prayers. As an embodied soul, you can't leave behind your body. (For a sweet exploration of body prayers, listen to Neil Douglas-Klotz's CD in *Blessings of the Cosmos*.)

You don't have to move your whole body. Mudras are highly effective, simple hand movements. The way I put my fingers together when I sing my conditions chant is a mudra. Mudras are good for your brain. When Andrew Newberg's clients sang a little meditative chant with simple finger movements, they demonstrated remarkable and rapid improvement in neural function. He concluded, "The addition of movement and singing to any meditation appears to significantly enhance the brain's performance. Our research suggests that the more complex you make your meditation, the more you enhance additional functions in the brain" (*How God Changes Your Brain*).

Sound

Make a joyful noise unto the Lord.

—Psalm 100:1

The Psalmists must have loved joyful noise. They encourage it in six Psalms. Well, you can make a joyful noise, too. Ring a bell, shake a rattle, tap a tambourine, clap your hands, knock two rocks together. Do something to awaken the sensation of sound. If you're deaf, hit a drum or play music with a lot of bass so you can feel the sound waves in your body. Add any sounds that feel joyful to you.

For a mind-boggling education on the mystical capacity of sound, visit *tomkenyon.com*. Tom Kenyon is a scientist, musician, mystic, and shaman—all wrapped around the beauty and power of sound. He has CDs of sounds for different purposes. *Infinite Pool* helps you experience the holographic universe. Doesn't that sound perfect for our mandala practice?

Smell and Taste

> *To eat a piece of bread or a bowl of rice mindfully and see that every morsel is a gift of the whole universe is to live deeply . . . When mindfulness is present, the Buddha and the Holy Spirit are already there.*
>
> —Thich Nhat Hanh, *Living Buddha, Living Christ*

To engage yourself at maximum capacity, you want to activate all your senses and fire up all your neurons. You see your mandala and all its delightful colors; you hear your voice and other sounds; you touch your mandala and move your body. Now watch what happens when you add smell and taste.

Smell is our most powerful sense. My favorite way to activate it is with fresh flowers and gently scented candles. I keep fresh lilies on my creative altar, but recently I added a mini-altar under my mandala. It has the crystal angel that sat on my mother's writing desk, an antique postcard with a stargazer lily, a nautilus shell, and a rose-scented "Manifest a Miracle" votive candle from Crystal Journey Candles. That pink candle wafts roses to me when I pray with my mandala and throughout the day.

Taste is perhaps our most outrageous sense. It surely belongs in embodied soul prayer. Begin with pure water. We know from Masaru Emoto's research and from Navajo tradition that water holds the energy of the words around it. Imagine how exquisite the molecule formation of your water is when you speak your mandala prayers. (In *Writing Down Your Soul*, you can read the story of why we drink water when we deep soul write.) You can also add a pure flower essence. I take an eye-dropper of the Lotus and the Lily flower essence from Green Hope Farms when I speak my prayers. It feels holy somehow to let the essence of lilies touch me in this intimate way.

But there's something else you can do. Add a pure food—something that delights your palate and speaks to you of your harvest. We are creating a life that generates delicious fruits, so perhaps a slice of apple or orange or one perfect blueberry is just the thing.

Create Your Mandala Ritual

Rituals add substance to our beliefs, and the more intense the ritual, the more likely we are to have a religious or spiritual epiphany.

—Andrew Newberg, *How God Changes Your Brain*

Take any of these suggestions and weave your own mandala prayer ritual. You can incorporate it into your existing spiritual practices or reserve it for another time of the day. I expanded my existing morning practice to include my mandala. Here's what I do: When I enter my office in the morning, I bless the space, walk to my altar, renew my soul vows, say my writing blessing, read Lorna Byrne's prayer from St. Michael and Lauren McLaughlin's twelve affirmations. Then I walk over to my mandala, make my declaration, speak with Spirit about what's happening, and chant my conditions. Last, I sit in my sacred writing chair and write down my soul. The whole practice takes twenty to thirty minutes—longer if I have a lot to say or a lot to write. For the astonishing benefits received, I'm amazed at the limited time invested. There is no set time frame, but Andrew Newberg's research found that twenty to forty minutes a day is the "ideal range of time to enhance the neural functioning of your brain."

But my mandala practice isn't restricted to the moments I stand in front of my mandala. It feeds me all day from its spot on the wall next to my computer. I catch myself staring at it often, especially when I'm searching for an idea or word. And if something upsets me, I look at my mandala and ask Spirit to help me get back to center. If I'm really upset, I'll jump up and sing my conditions again. I also keep a copy of my mandala on my bedroom wall, where it feeds me all night and is often the first thing I see when I wake.

Others place their mandala in their bedroom and pray with it every morning and night. Others place it in a central hallway or in multiple spots around the house, where they can visit them throughout the day. Some make a mini version and keep it in a frame at work and say their prayers in the car. Others convert a photo of their mandala into a screensaver and whisper their conditions whenever it appears. Linda Bryant made a big mandala in her Nashville home and a tiny travel mandala to take with her when she traveled to London for her MFA classes. Jazz Jaeschke set up a traveling altar complete with mini mandala, rocks, and candles on a finger-labyrinth cloth.

Only you can decide how you want to work with your mandala and when and where. Those details aren't important, but creating a ritual and committing to it is. In *How God Changes Your Brain,* Newberg stresses the benefits of daily spiritual practice: "Five minutes of prayer once a week may have little effect, but forty minutes of daily practice, over a period of years, will bring permanent changes to the brain." So have a lovely time creating your unique mandala prayer ritual and incorporating it into your life.

Take Three Steps

However many holy words you read, however many you speak, what good will they do you if you do not act upon them?

—The Buddha

Your mandala is spinning and attracting; your seeds are sprouting. What's left for you to do? Three things.

First, keep your mandala and all your spiritual practices alive. Refresh your spiritual life every day or as often as you can. Don't let weeks go by without feeding your soul. If you do, your land will begin to feel parched. If that should happen, don't be discouraged; just return and begin anew.

Second, live your conditions. This doesn't mean just say the words. Living your conditions means filtering all your choices and actions and decisions through the essence and meaning of those commitments. When you do that, decisions get easier. You know almost immediately what belongs in your world and what doesn't. As you do this consistently, your whole life gets easier. Not only because you know what to do and why, but also because your intentions resonate so strongly within your choices that, like little tuning forks, they attract only that which vibrates at the same philosophical and moral pitch. Situations that might have been a wrestling match before simply fade away or don't show up or resolve themselves.

There's a third step that emphatically reinforces and supports the soul-directed life you are creating: take action. A famous Sufi saying is, "Take one earnest step towards your heartfelt dream, and your heartfelt dream will take 10 steps towards you. Take another earnest step and your dream takes 100 steps towards you." Goethe puts it this way, "Whatever you can do or dream you can, begin it. Boldness has genius, power and magic in it!"

The soul is a wonderful creator, and often the work of creation is effortless, but taking one little step of initiation can open a floodgate of opportunity. I experienced this on May 15, 2007. I was frustrated because my book contract was six months delayed. I was listening to a talk online, and the speaker said, "What would you be doing right now, if you knew what you wanted was coming on Friday?" I grabbed a pen and wrote three pages of things I'd be doing. At the top of the list was "write my writing blessing," and that afternoon I wrote it. The next morning, May 16, I stood in front of my altar and spoke my writing blessing aloud for the first time. Two days later, the doorbell rang. It was the Fed Ex delivery person bearing an envelope containing my book contract—dated May 16.

Whenever someone feels stuck, I tell her this story and ask, "What would you be doing right now if you knew what you wanted was coming on Friday?" In the midst of the housing crisis in Florida, a friend complained his house wouldn't sell. I asked the question, and he answered, "Well geez, I'd be packing." He went home and started packing. His house sold in sixty days.

Take a step toward your dreams and watch how your dreams take a step to you. That's partnership.

Collect Your Evidence

"To receive we must be alert, awake and prepared to receive. Above all, persons should at all times be prepared for the gifts of God and always prepare themselves anew. For God is a thousand times more eager to give than we are to receive."

—Meister Eckhart, *Breakthrough:*
Meister Eckhart's Creation Spirituality in New Translation, Matthew Fox

How will you know if your mandala is working? How can you tell if your conditions are nourishing your seeds and your seeds are growing? Well, the truth is, you can't miss it. Things happen. Help arrives. The phone rings. Introductions are made. Information comes. Friends appear. Work falls out of the sky. Love blooms. Ideas enter. Problems dissolve. Health returns. Suits are settled. Tests are passed. Money shows up. Debts are erased. Surprises and synchronicities simply abound.

All you have to do is pay attention and collect evidence. In *Writing Down Your Soul,* I suggest you set up an evidence shelf and store on it all the signs of your divine partner moving in your life. For the Lotus and the Lily, you can track your evidence even more closely and compare it to your mandala.

A lovely way to collect your evidence is to make a blank wheel about the same size as your mandala. At the end of each month, have a special deep soul writing conversation. Review all that happened in the last thirty days. Make a list of all the evidence, big and small, that your seeds are growing. And don't overlook the seeds that sprang up even though you didn't consciously plant them. They are such delightful surprises and sweet reminders that when we create a condition of receptivity, we don't even have to ask.

Look at all your evidence for the month and come up with a phrase or image that captures the gifts of the month. Record that in the one o'clock position on your blank evidence wheel. At the end of twelve months, you'll have an astonishing record of how living your conditions has changed your life. Jazz Jaeschke was one of the first to make an evidence wheel. You don't have to know what her pictures mean; you can't miss the power of all that evidence accumulating over a year. Jazz said this is a powerful reminder of how beautiful life can be when you give the soul all the room and all the tools it needs to create a beautiful, abundant life.

Jazz Jaeschke, Evidence Wheel

Negative Evidence

But when you run up against the hard edge and have to stand true to
love anyway, what emerges is the most precious taste of pure divine love.

—Cynthia Bourgeault, *The Wisdom Jesus*

What if you don't get what you want? This may well be one of
the most beautiful and mysterious aspects of creating a life in
concert with the Divine. You focus on creating your conditions, and you take steps toward what you want, but sometimes
nothing happens. Or something quite different than what you
expect happens. Sometimes it feels like the road swerved or
changed or dumped you in a strange new land. Does this mean
the mandala didn't work? Did it attract the wrong thing? Did
the masters miss something in their teachings?

No, it means that you are doubly blessed—blessed by what
you receive *and* blessed by what you do not. There are powers
directing your gifts, both the ones that look delightful and the
ones that don't. These powers begin inside of you, in your
soul—your great mysterious, glorious soul. One of your soul's
powers is knowing and planning on a plane you don't have
access to in human consciousness. The mind is powerful, but
it does not and cannot see the whole picture.

When Job complained to Yahweh about his life, Yahweh
assaulted him with a barrage of unanswerable and truly exquisite questions:

Where were you when I laid the earth's foundations?
(Job 38:4)

Have you ever in your life given orders to the morning?
(Job 38:12)

Have you visited the place where the snow is stored?
(Job 38:22)

Can you fasten the harness of the Pleiades, or untie Orion's bands? (Job 38:31)

After a torrent of these questions, Job humbly responded: My words have been frivolous: what can I reply? I had better lay my hand over my mouth. (Job 40:4)

Like Job, you do not direct everything that happens in this vast and glorious universe. Nor does your soul. Nor do your angels or your guides. But your soul and your angels and your guides do have a view of a bigger picture: why you came and what you really want at the soul level. What a comfort it is to know that there is a part of you that already knows. Your soul knows, your angels know, your guides know, the Divine knows, and all are working with you to create a life filled with real beauty and real abundance. This is the authentic life you want. This is the life that moves you gently and always toward your ultimate goal—wholeness.

Paradox Alert:
Not getting what you want
can be getting exactly what you want.

So when things work out differently than you expect, stop and look at where you are. Visualize your human self *inside* your mandala and your divine team and soul self *outside* your mandala, seeing the vast black space and all the unlimited potential. Then bless the gifts you have received and bless the gifts you have not. Even if you're not certain what is happening or what it means or where it's all going, trust that your wild soul does, and say thank you. Then watch what happens. It may be a surprise—and a beautiful one at that.

A Year with a Mandala

I've shared with you the dramatic results of living with my 2010 and 2011 Intention Mandalas: "My Breakthrough Year" and "Big Pot." Here, in their own words, are the stories of three women who created Intention Mandalas in 2010 and what happened as a result.

Jazz Jaeschke (Austin, Texas)

After living with "Harmony Happens" (see page 187) for a year, Jazz shared a few of her experiences.

> I felt a travel trailer could promote harmony by lessening the hassle of traveling with my partner and our dog. I stuck a suitable image on my mandala. A month later, my partner suggested we might visit the Casita factory, three hours north of us. Turns out the picture I snagged was a Casita and matches the trailer that's now in our driveway. We spent five weeks in seventeen feet of trailer without one emotional eruption. That's harmony.
>
> I think the universe granted one specific request to nurture my confidence. I also asked for elbow room in my writing space, using a picture of people with elbows bumping. I thought I'd have to add on to the house or rent space. But one day I realized clearing clutter would reclaim elbow room aplenty.
>
> All year long, requests materialized, and harmony really did happen.

Catherine Anderson (Charlotte, North Carolina)

Catherine Anderson spoke about living with her mandala, "My Year of Connecting with Mystical Wisdom" (see page 198)

> When I made my mandala, I didn't really know what I meant by "connecting with mystical wisdom"—it just felt

right. But it seems that my inner knowing/soul already knew what lay ahead. My mandala came to life in many more ways than I could have expected. So much happened to lead me along that path. Wisdom University offered a week-long intensive with Jean Houston on "Women Mystics and the Mystical Path to Creativity." Then I participated in a 13 Moons intensive about claiming my power and my priestess energy, and I recently went on a pilgrimage to Teotihuacan, Mexico, which was a mystical experience. None of these things were available when I made my mandala, so I wasn't sure how I was going to fulfill my intention.

And my book, *The Creative Photographer,* was published this year. That was quite a surprise. I visualized myself holding my published book and giving thanks, then I sent the proposal. It was a Tuesday, and on Thursday the publisher contacted me to say they were interested. That's magic. There's no other word for it.

Beth Reilly (Bradenton, Florida)

Beth Reilly's mandala, "A Year of Living Deeply," (see page 196) held a few surprises.

My mandala is in my bedroom, on top of my spiritual library bookcase-altar. When I look at it, it centers me. As my eyes travel around the mandala, inner responses range from "Oh, yes" to "I'm there" to "I'm still working on this." Frequently I find the photos lead me to a deeper level, even after a year and half, revealing perspectives, gifts, and challenges I didn't see even a week ago.

It was quite powerful when I looked at the joy of the dancer in the School section and compared it with how I felt at the end of the first semester of my doctorate program. My soul had clearly communicated its need regarding education. The doctorate was not feeding my soul. I resigned. The classes I'm now taking in art do feed my soul. I can now look at that dancer and feel her joy.

I'd placed an abdomen in Health without knowing why. Several months later, I discovered a serious issue in my digestive tract.

I love the woman walking on the path in Self-Discovery. After gazing at her for many months, I realized she's wearing a robe they give you in a spa, so pleasure is always present.

The woman in Live Deeply still speaks on so many levels to me. She sees, hears, and feels the energy of life and her soul. I now consider her a guide, and she will be incorporated in the next mandala.

Keep Your Intention Mandala Alive

We are fellow-helpers with God,
co-creators in everything we do.
When Word and work are returned to their source and origin
then all work is accomplished divinely in God.
And there too
the soul loses itself
in a wonderful enchantment.

—Meister Eckhart, *Meditations with Meister Eckhart,* Matthew Fox

Like Jazz, Catherine, and Beth, as you live with your Intention Mandala, you, too, will discover what it means and what your soul was saying when it selected those shapes and colors and images and words. You, too, will stand in awe of how your soul creates a beautiful, abundant life. The magic is just beginning.

But as you live with your mandala and live your conditions, you'll make the most amazing discovery: it isn't magic after all. It is, just as the masters taught, the natural order. Conditions first, manifestation second. One flows naturally from the other. Create the fertile soil, and you create a condition of receptivity in which the seeds you plant grow lushly alongside the delightful and unexpected seeds your divine team drops when you're not looking.

The result? Heaven on earth. Does this heaven mean material things? Well, the garden is lush, so yes, the harvest can be tangible. But its greatest gifts are not held in your hands. They are held in your heart. First among them is the intimate relationship with creation itself—Jung's "Eternal Mind's eternal recreation." What a treasure it is to know how to live in concert with the miraculous and playful creative forces of life. When you know how to play this divine game, endless struggle comes to an end. Another priceless gift is walking this earth knowing you are living the life your soul wants to create. Another is the sheer joy of watching your garden grow, knowing you are creating it in partnership with the Divine and according to spiritual law. The gifts are boundless, unfolding in richer and more marvelous ways with each passing day.

Perhaps the greatest gift of all is friendship with the mystery at the center of it all. Put out a welcome mat for paradox and wonder and mystery, and life only gets more amazing. Einstein said he wanted to know the thoughts of God. He must have gotten a peek, because he said, "The most beautiful thing we can experience is the mysterious. He . . . who can no longer pause to wonder and stand rapt in awe, is as good as dead: his eyes are closed."

Our eyes are open, wide open, in wonder. Or, as Meister Eckhart prefers, enchantment. And for this mystery, this enchantment, we can only be grateful. What else is there to feel or express?

And So, We Say Farewell

We began in intention, and we end in gratitude, the holy twins of soul exploration. We have learned from the masters, stepped into the mystery, and, in concert with our souls, begun to create heaven on earth. And all is well. We end where we began, in the wise arms of the English mystic, Julian of Norwich, who knew in the fourteenth century what we are learning now: "All shall be well and all shall be well and all manner of thing shall be well."

Nourish

I pray with 100 percent of my being.
I nourish my beautiful life.

Want More?

Today is a beginning, not an ending. You now know how to tune into the wisdom of your soul and, in concert with that wisdom, create a whole, beautiful, abundant life. To nourish that life, gather around you a rich soul library you can turn to over and over again. In the "Resources" section you will find many of the books and tools I love.

acknowledgments

There are many hands and hearts between the covers of *The Lotus and the Lily*. Some are evident, but most are not. I bow to them all. I bow first in gratitude to the brilliant team at Conari Press: Jan Johnson, who said a very big yes; Susie Pitzen, who walked so gently beside me; and Jim Warner, who once again captured the essence of my book in his eloquent cover. I bow to the marketing team, Bonni Hamilton, Pat Rose, and Lisa Trudeau, who bang the drum with such style and grace. I bow deeply to my divinely appointed editor, Amy Rost, in whose hands my threads are woven into silk. If you love the way this book sounds, bow to her, too. Heart-to-heart, I bend toward Nancy Barton. I drew "my perfect agent" on my 2010 Intention Mandala and heaven said, "Here you go." And I bow to Jo Ann Deck, the best publishing consultant a writer could ask for.

I bow with particular joy to the original members of "The Lotus and the Lily" telecourses who threw themselves into this unknown and unheralded process, created their Intention Mandalas, and shared their miraculous results. All of your spirits are alive in this book. Particular blessings to Jazz Jaeschke, Beth Reilly, and Catherine Anderson, who generously shared their mandalas and their stories. Thanks to you, the world can see how beautiful and miraculous an Intention Mandala can be.

My heart is filled with gratitude for all who sustained me during the intense months of writing: my son, Jerry, who loves me so much he didn't come home for Christmas; my sister and brother-in-law, Claire and Bob, who kept the pantry full; and my brother, Larry, who understood instantly the implications of the mandala. I am grateful to have two gifted women in my life: Margo Mastromarchi, through whom the angels speak, and Lauralyn Bunn, through whom the masters and teachers of the Akashic Record deliver both their profound wisdom and their delicious sense of humor. And I bow to Cherry Lea, who always calls at exactly the right moment with exactly what I need to hear. I don't know what divine contract we have, Cherry, but it's a doozy!

But above all, I bow to two teachers, Thich Nhat Hanh, who planted the Buddha in my heart in just one sentence, and Neil Douglas-Klotz, who introduced me to the Jesus I always wanted to know. I cannot recommend their work enough. And, of course, I bow to my dear friend, Hafiz, who talks to me at every turn, whether I want to hear what he has to say or not.

And last, but always first, I pour myself out before the One, the Center, the Source of all. After all these years, I still stare in wonder when you speak on my pages. I hope this book has served you well. I am deeply, deeply blessed.

Janet Conner
Ozona, Florida
May 11, 2012

resources

Nourish Review

Here are all thirty-two of the nourishing spiritual truths you absorbed during this program. Review this list every month or so to replenish your spiritual fields.

Week 1: Prepare

1. I am a spiritual being with the power of intention.
2. I am not alone. I have a loving spiritual support team.
3. I am my own shaman. I have direct and immediate access to Spirit.
4. I create my own lifting rituals.
5. I pray.
6. I transmute doubt and fear.
7. I stop and savor my life.

Week 2: Look Back

8. I look for and find the gifts in my life.
9. I am the main character in my life's movie.
10. I receive messages from Spirit and my guides all the time.
11. I release my thought worms.
12. I choose to not go back to sleep.
13. I am a spark of the Divine.
14. I say thank you for all.

Week 3: Create Space

15. I untie the knot, and I am free.

16. I release what is dead, and the vultures take it away.

17. I forgive myself.

18. I am enough.

19. I release my prisoners.

20. I choose to forgive.

21. I totally and completely forgive myself.

Week 4: Look Forward

22. I am a powerful being with the power to create.

23. My soul has a purpose.

24. I see my beautiful future.

25. I decide to trust.

26. I fill my cart with the desires of my soul.

27. I name my future.

28. I focus only on what's coming in.

Soul Day Preparation

29. I prepare to create with the Divine.

Soul Day

30. I create with the Divine.

Keep It Alive

31. I pray with 100 percent of my being.

32. I nourish my beautiful life.

paradox alerts review

Paradox is the language through which
God communicates with us.

—Caroline Myss, *Entering the Castle*

Another way to replenish your fields is to sit with paradox. Here are the paradoxical gifts you received throughout this program. By no means is this a comprehensive list. It's just a small taste to help you become aware of the rich gifts of paradox.

- You can have anything you want but not by wanting.
- The present is made up of the past and the future, and the past and the future are in the present.
- You may feel the greatest gratitude for your most difficult gifts.
- If you forgive with the intention of manipulating another person's behavior, it's not forgiveness.
- You don't want any thing; you want the freedom the thing can produce.
- Look for the extraordinary in the ordinary.
- When you hold others prisoner, you hold yourself prisoner.
- The path to trust is trust.
- Not getting what you want can be getting exactly what you want.

your soul wants
five things

"Your Soul Wants Five Things" is Janet Conner's complete learning series addressing the five essential desires of the soul. Janet teaches the five courses live once every year. *Writing Down Your Soul* and *The Lotus and the Lily* are now available as books from Conari Press. Janet is currently working on the rest of the books in the series.

Your Soul Wants To:	Book and Course	Wisdom Habit Developed
1. connect with Source	*Writing Down Your Soul*	deep soul writing
2. commit to values	*Soul Vows*	daily renewal of your soul's most precious values
3. serve a purpose	*Check the Box*	a life aligned with your soul's unique purpose
4. express itself	*Plug In for Writers* *Plug In for Expressive Souls*	working in the inter-section between craft and spiritual practice
5. create life	*The Lotus and the Lily*	Intention Mandala and daily mandala prayer practice

books, people, and websites

Spiritual Masters

The Buddha

Chodron, Pema. *The Places That Scare You: A Guide to Fearlessness in Difficult Times* (Shambhala, 2001).

Gattuso, Joan. *The Lotus Still Blooms: Sacred Buddhist Teachings for the Western Mind* (Jeremy P. Tarcher/Penguin, 2008).

Hanh, Thich Nhat. *The Heart of the Buddha's Teachings: Transforming Suffering into Peace, Joy, and Liberation* (Broadway Books, 1998).

Hanh, Thich Nhat. *You Are Here: Discovering the Magic of the Present Moment* (Shambhala Publications, 2009).

His Holiness the Dalai Lama. *The Dalai Lama's Little Book of Wisdom: The Essential Teachings* (Hampton Roads, 2009).

Jesus

Borg, Marcus. *Meeting Jesus Again for the First Time: The Historical Jesus & The Heart of Contemporary Faith* (HarperCollins, 1994).

Bourgeault, Cynthia. *The Wisdom Jesus: Transforming Heart and Mind—a New Perspective on Christ and His Message* (Shambhala, 2008).

Chopra, Deepak. *The Third Jesus: The Christ We Cannot Ignore* (Three Rivers Press, 2008).

Douglas-Klotz, Neil. *Blessings of the Cosmos: Wisdom of the Heart from the Aramaic Words of Jesus* (Sounds True, 2006).

Douglas-Klotz, Neil. *The Hidden Gospel: Decoding the Spiritual Message of the Aramaic Jesus* (Quest Books, 1999).

Douglas-Klotz, Neil. *Prayers of the Cosmos: Meditations on the Aramaic Words of Jesus* (HarperCollins, 1990).

For more on Neil Douglas-Klotz, visit the Abwoon Resource Center (*abwoon.com*).

Errico, Rocco A. *Setting a Trap for God: The Aramaic Prayer of Jesus* (Unity Books, 1997).

Errico, Rocco A. and Nina Shabaz. *Aramaic Light on the Gospel of Matthew* (Noohra Foundation, 2000).

For more on Dr. Errico's research, visit the Noohra Foundation at *noohra. com* or his personal website, *roccoaerrico.com*.

Parallel Teachings of the Buddha and Jesus

Borg, Marcus. *Jesus & Buddha: The Parallel Sayings* (Ulysses Press, 2004).

Hanh, Thich Nhat. *Living Buddha Living Christ: 10th Anniversary Edition* (Riverhead Books, 2007).

Hooper, Richard. *Jesus, Buddha, Krishna & Lao Tzu: The Parallel Sayings* (Hampton Roads, 2012).

Bibles and Gospels

Borg, Marcus. *The Lost Gospel: The Original Sayings of Jesus* (Ulysses Press, 1996).

Funk, Robert W., Roy W. Hoover, and the Jesus Seminar. *The Five Gospels: What Did Jesus Really Say? The Search for the Authentic Words of Jesus* (HarperCollins, 1993).

Holy Bible from the Ancient Eastern Text: George M. Lamsa's *Translations from the Aramaic of the Peshitta* (HarperOne; original copyright by A. J. Holman Company, 1933).

Meyer, Marvin. *The Gospels of Mary: The Secret Tradition of Mary Magdalene the Companion of Jesus* (HarperOne, 2004).

The New Jerusalem Bible, Reader's Edition (Doubleday, 1990).

Wisdom from the East and Middle East

Douglas-Klotz, Neil. *Desert Wisdom; Sacred Middle Eastern Writings from the Goddess Through the Sufis* (Harper San Francisco, 1995).

Douglas-Klotz, Neil. *The Sufi Book of Life: 99 Pathways of the Heart for the Modern Dervish* (Penguin, 2005).

Nouwen, Henri. *The Way of the Heart: The Spirituality of the Desert Fathers and Mothers* (HarperOne, 1991).

Osho. *Zen: The Path of Paradox* (St Martin's Griffin, 2001).

Tao Te Ching (Jeremy P. Tarcher/Penguin, 2008), translation by Jonathan Star.

Tao Te Ching: A New English Translation (Harper Perennial Modern Classics, 2006), translation by Stephen Mitchell.

Yogananda, Paramahansa. *Autobiography of a Yogi* (Self-Realization Fellowship, 2007).

The Life of the Soul

Conner, Janet. *My Soul Pages: A Companion to Writing Down Your Soul* (Conari Press, 2011).

Conner, Janet. *Writing Down Your Soul: How to Activate and Listen to the Extraordinary Voice Within* (Conari Press, 2009).

Goldsmith, Joel. *The Contemplative Life* (Martino Fine Books, 2010 reprint of 1963 edition).

Goldsmith, Joel. *Practicing the Presence: The Inspirational Guide to Regaining Meaning and a Sense of Purpose in Your Life* (HarperOne, 1991).

Moore, Thomas. *Care of the Soul: A Guide for Cultivating Depth and Sacredness in Everyday Life* (reprint edition; Harper Perennial, 1994).

Myss, Caroline. *Entering the Castle: An Inner Path to God and Your Soul* (Free Press, 2007).

Myss, Caroline. *Spiritual Madness: The Necessity of Meeting God in Darkness* (audiobook; Sounds True, 2002).

O'Donohue, John. *Anam Cara: A Book of Celtic Wisdom* (HarperCollins, 1998).

O'Donohue, John. *Beauty: The Invisible Embrace* (Harper Perennial, 2005).

Rohr, Richard. *The Naked Now: Learning to See as the Mystics See* (The Crossroad Publishing Company, 2009).

Zukav, Gary. *The Seat of the Soul* (Free Press, 1990).

The Intersection of Spirituality and Science

Childre, Doc, and Howard Martin. *The Heartmath Solution: The Institute of HeartMath's Revolutionary Program for Engaging the Power of the Heart's Intelligence* (HarperOne, 2000).

Davidson, Richard J., and Jon Kabat-Zinn, eds. *The Mind's Own Physician: A Scientific Dialogue with the Dalai Lama on the Healing Power of Meditation* (New Harbinger, 2012).

Dossey, Larry. *Prayer Is Good Medicine: How to Reap the Healing Benefits of Prayer* (HarperOne, 1997).

Dossey, Larry. *Reinventing Medicine Beyond Mind-Body to a New Era of Healing* (HarperOne, 2000).

Hagerty, Barbara Bradley. *The Fingerprints of God: What Science Is Learning about the Brain and Spiritual Experience* (Riverhead Trade, 2010).

McTaggart, Lynne. *The Bond: Connecting Through the Space Between Us* (Free Press, 2011).

McTaggart, Lynne. *The Intention Experiment: Using Your Thoughts to Change Your Life and the World* (Free Press, 2008).

Newberg, Andrew. *Principles of Neurotheology* (Ashgate, 2010).

Newberg, Andrew, and Mark Robert Waldman. *How God Changes Your Brain: Breakthrough Findings from a Leading Neuroscientist* (Ballantine Books, 2010).

The Akashic Field and Akashic Record

Lauralyn Bunn, Akashic reader trainer and guide, Akashic Pathways (*akashicpathways.com*)

Howe, Linda. *How to Read the Akashic Records: Accessing the Archive of the Soul and Its Journey* (Sounds True, 2010).

Laszlo, Ervin. *Science and the Akashic Field: An Integral Theory of Everything* (2nd edition, Inner Traditions, 2007).

McTaggert, Lynne. *The Field: The Quest for the Secret Force of the Universe* (Harper Perennial, 2008).

Ritual

Campbell, Joseph, with Bill Moyers. *The Power of Myth* (Anchor, 1991).

Somé, Malidoma Patrice. *Of Water and the Spirit: Ritual, Magic and Initiation in the Life of an African Shaman* (Penguin, 1995).

Mystical Poetry and Mystics

Fox, Matthew. *Breakthrough: Meister Eckhart's Creation Spirituality in New Translation* (Image Books, Doubleday, 1980).

Fox, Matthew. *Meditations with Meister Eckhart* (Bear & Company, 1983).

Julian of Nowrich, *Revelation of Love* (Image Books, Doubleday, 1996), John Skinner, ed., trans.

Ladinsky, Daniel. *The Gift: Poems by Hafiz the Great Sufi Master* (Penguin, 1999).

Ladinsky, Daniel. *I Heard God Laughing: Poems of Hope and Joy* (Penguin, 2006).

Ladinsky, Daniel. *Love Poems from God: Twelve Sacred Voices from East and West* (Penguin, 2002).

Ladinsky, Daniel. *The Subject Tonight Is Love: 60 Wild and Sweet Poems of Hafiz* (Penguin, 2003).

Ladinsky, Daniel. *A Year with Hafiz: Daily Contemplations* (Penguin, 2011).

Rumi, Jalal al-Din. *The Essential Rumi: New Expanded Edition* (HarperOne, 2004), Coleman Barks, trans.

Whyte, David. *The House of Belonging* (Many Rivers Press, 1997).

Forgiveness

Brown, Brene. *The Gifts of Imperfection: Let Go of Who You Think You're Supposed to Be and Embrace Who You Are* (Hazelden, 2010).

Grieco, Mary Hayes. *Unconditional Forgiveness: A Simple and Proven Method to Forgive Everyone and Everything* (Atria Books/Beyond Words, 2011).

Tipping, Colin. *Radical Forgiveness: A Revolutionary Five-Stage Process to Heal Relationshihps, Let Go of Anger and Blame, Find Peace in Any Situation* (Sounds True, 2009).

Gratefulness

Ryan, M. J., ed. *A Grateful Heart: Daily Blessings for the Evening Meal from Buddha to the Beatles* (Conari Press, 1994).

Steindl-Rast, David. *Gratefulness, the Heart of Prayer: An Approach to Life in Fullness* (Paulist Press, 1984).

Sacred Geometry

Hart, Francene. *Sacred Geometry Oracle Deck* (Bear & Company, 2001).

Mandalas

Arguelles, Jose and Miriam Arguelles. *Mandala,* foreword by Chogyam Trungpa (Shambhala, 1972; out of print).

Brauen, Martin. *Mandala: Sacred Circle in Tibetan Buddhism* (Arnoldsche Verlagsanstalt, 2009).

Cunningham, Bailey. *Mandala: Journey to the Center* (DK Adult Whole Way Library, 2003; out of print).

Cunningham, Bailey. *The Mandala Book: Patterns of the Universe* (Sterling, 2010).

Jung, C. G. *Mandala Symbolism* (Princeton University Press, 1972; out of print).

Jung, C. G. *Memories, Dreams, Reflections* (Vintage, 1989).

Jung, C. G. *Psychology and Alchemy: Collected Works of C. G. Jung, Vol. 12* (Princeton University Press, 1980).

The Mandala Project, (*mandalaproject.org*, inactive site).

Eileen Rose, mandala artist, Illuminated Rose (*illuminatedrose.com*) and Mandala Illumination (*mandalaillumination.com*).

Lillian Sizemore, mosaic mandala artist, *lilliansizemore.com*

Thurman, Robert, and Denise Patry Leidy. *Mandala: The Architecture of Enlightenment* (Overlook TP, 2006; out of print).

Angels

Bryne, Lorna. *Angels in My Hair: The True Story of a Modern-Day Irish Mystic* (Three Rivers Press, 2011).

Bryne, Lorna. *Stairways to Heaven* (Coronet, 2011).

Lorna Byrne, *lornabyrne.com*

Margo Mastromarchi, angel guidance reader, Oracle of the Dove (*oracleofthedove.com*)

Virtue, Doreen. *Archangel Oracle Cards* (Hay House, 2004). (Doreen Virtue also has many other books and decks on angels.)

Animal and Other Messengers

Andrews, Ted. *Animal Speak: The Spiritual & Magical Powers of Creatures Great & Small* (Llewellyn, 2002).

Blum, Ralph H. *The Book of Runes 25th Anniversary Edition* (Thomas Dunne Books, 2008).

Sams, Jamie, David Carson, and Angela Werneke. *Medicine Cards: The Discovery of Power Through the Ways of Animals* (St Martin's Press, 1999).

Virtue, Doreen. *Goddess Guidance Oracle Cards* (Hay House, 2004).

Flower Essences

Green Hope Farm Flower Essences, *greenhopeessences.com*. Ask for the custom-designed flower essence for "The Lotus and the Lily," listed under "Combination Collection," as well as other essences for all five courses in the "Your Soul Wants Five Things" series.

Music

Theta Music CD by Solarzar, available at *janetconner.com*.

The Ghandarva Experience CD (Tom Kenyon/ORB Communications), *tomkenyon.com*

Deva Premal, *devapremalmiten.com*
Gregorian or Byzantine chants
Hildegard of Bingen chants

JanetConner.com

Hear or watch all the poems, prayers, and guided meditations in this book. See people's mandalas and read their stories—and share your own. Learn more about the "Your Soul Wants Five Things" series. Subscribe to Janet's newsletter.

permissions

Poems and excerpts from Daniel Ladinsky's translations are from the Penguin publications *The Gift: Poems by Hafiz* ©1999 Daniel Ladinsky; *The Subject Tonight Is Love: 60 Wild and Sweet Poems of Hafiz* ©1996 & 2003 Daniel Ladinsky; *Love Poems from God: Twelve Sacred Voices from the East and West* ©2002 Daniel Ladinsky; *I Heard God Laughing: Poems of Hope and Joy* ©1996 & 2006 Daniel Ladinsky and used with his permission.

Neil Douglas-Klotz, excerpts from *Blessings of the Cosmos.* Copyright © 2006 by Neil Douglas-Klotz. Reprinted with the permission of Sounds True, Inc.

Meditations with Meister Eckhart Edited by Matthew Fox, published by Bear & Company, a division of Inner Traditions International, 1983. All rights reserved. innertraditions.com Reprinted with permission of publisher.

Laozi, excerpt from Verse 74 from *Tao Te Ching: A New English Version*, translated by Stephen Mitchell. Copyright © 1988 by Stephen Mitchell. Reprinted by permission of HarperCollins Publishers.

Andrew Newberg, MD, excerpts from *How God Changes Your Brain: Breakthrough Findings from a Leading Neuroscientist.* Copyright © 2009 by Andrew Newberg, MD. Used by permission of Ballantine Books, a division of Random House, Inc.

Rumi, excerpt from "The breeze at dawn . . ." from *The Essential Rumi*, translated by Coleman Barks (New York: HarperCollins, 2004). Copyright © 1995, 2004 by Coleman Barks. Reprinted with the permission of the translator.

Thich Nhat Hanh, excerpts from *You Are Here: Discovering the Magic of the Present Moment.* Copyright © 2009. Reprinted with the permission of Shambhala Publications, Inc.

about the author

Janet Conner is a vibrant writer, speaker, and teacher who became a catalyst for deep soul change after a series of personal traumas. Her landmark book, *Writing Down Your Soul* (Conari Press, 2009), connects readers to their "extraordinary voice within" and is consistently a five-star rated, top-ranked book in the journal-writing category. Janet and her work have been featured in national media including *Martha Stewart's Whole Living*, *Daily Word*, *Daily Om*, *Beliefnet.com*, and more. Janet lives in Ozona, Florida; speaks nationally at conferences, churches, book events, and retreats; and teaches a series of sell-out telecourses with thousands of students worldwide. With her signature teaching of "Your Soul Wants Five Things," Janet is fast becoming a major voice for spiritual growth and understanding in our time.

to our readers

Conari Press, an imprint of Red Wheel/Weiser, publishes books on topics ranging from spirituality, personal growth, and relationships to women's issues, parenting, and social issues. Our mission is to publish quality books that will make a difference in people's lives—how we feel about ourselves and how we relate to one another. We value integrity, compassion, and receptivity, both in the books we publish and in the way we do business.

Our readers are our most important resource, and we appreciate your input, suggestions, and ideas about what you would like to see published.

Visit our website at *www.redwheelweiser.com* to learn about our upcoming books and free downloads, and be sure to go to *www.redwheelweiser.com/newsletter/* to sign up for newsletters and exclusive offers.

You can also contact us at info@redwheelweiser.com.

Conari Press
an imprint of Red Wheel/Weiser, LLC
665 Third Street, Suite 400
San Francisco, CA 94107